Contents

People in the story

Marilyn Whittle – Harp

Frank Shepherd – Orchestra Manager

Adriana Fox – Violin

Martin Audley – Trumpet

Philip Worth – Conductor

Penny Wade – Double Bass

Simon Hunt – Double Bass

Candida Ashley-Morton – Double Bass

Inspector Jorge Portillo

Chapter 1 *A bit of a problem*

We came out of the airport building. All eighty-five players from the Barston Symphony Orchestra in England. The sun was shining. It was hot.

'Welcome to Barcelona!' Frank Shepherd said to us all. 'Come this way. The coaches are waiting.' We followed him. Somebody took a photograph.

The coaches left the airport and started on the motorway into Barcelona. Frank Shepherd came and sat next to me. Frank is the manager of the Barston Symphony Orchestra.

'Penny,' he said (that's my name). 'We've got a bit of a problem.'

'What kind of a problem?' I said.

'Well, it's your double bass,' he said.

'My double bass? What's wrong with my double bass?'

'It isn't here. It isn't in Barcelona.'

'What? Where is it?'

'I'm afraid that I just don't know,' Frank said.

Oh, sorry. I must tell you something about me because, well, this is my story. Actually that's not quite true. It's the story of a double bass too. People take things and somebody dies. But that's for later. Now I'll start at the beginning.

My name is Penny Wade. I am twenty-six years old. I play the double bass in the Barston Symphony Orchestra. There are eight double basses in the BSO. I am number eight. I got the job six months ago. The other seven players are all older or better than me. The trip to Spain was my first time with the orchestra in a foreign country.

'What's the problem?' my friend Adriana said from the seat behind me. Adriana plays the violin in the orchestra.

'It's my double bass,' I said. 'Frank can't find it.'

'I'm sorry,' Frank said. 'We put it in the BSO truck in Barston and it wasn't in the truck when it arrived in Barcelona.'

All the big instruments came by road. It was cheaper than taking them in a plane.

'He says someone's taken it,' I told Adriana.

'I said *perhaps* someone's taken it,' Frank said.

'That's no help at all,' I said. I was angry. '*Perhaps* isn't any good. Perhaps it fell off the truck. Perhaps someone wanted wood for their fire . . . '

'Look,' Adriana said. 'This is stupid. Double basses are big. They don't just fall off trucks.'

'This one did,' I said. I looked out of the window of the coach. We were arriving in Barcelona. My first foreign trip. Wonderful, don't you think? But that's just the problem. It wasn't wonderful at all.

Chapter 2 *A beautiful day*

I woke up. I looked around me. Where was I? Then I remembered. I was in a hotel in Barcelona. With the Barston Symphony Orchestra. But without my double bass.

I went to the dining room and had coffee. Simon Hunt was at my table. I was his girlfriend, and he was my boyfriend. I think.

'Listen,' he said. 'You know tonight's concert.'

'Yes,' I said, 'and I can't play in it.'

'Well, you can if you want,' he smiled. 'You can play in my place.'

'Oh Simon, really?'

'Yes, I've hurt my hand, so ... erm ... I can't play, you see.'

I looked at his hand. I couldn't see anything wrong.

'It looks OK,' I said.

'Well, it isn't,' he answered quickly.

I liked Simon very much. He was tall and handsome. He had dark hair and blue eyes. He was double bass number two in our orchestra and ten years older than me.

'Are you all right?' I put my hand on his arm.

'I'll be fine.' He took my hand away. 'I've talked to Candida about tonight.' (Candida was the leader of the double basses.) 'She says it's OK.'

'Thanks, Simon.'

'Yes, well, it's nothing. It means that I get a free afternoon.'

'Well, we're both free this morning,' I said. 'We can do something together.'

'Hmmm,' he said.

'Perhaps we can go to the Picasso museum. Or the Parc Güell? Or up to Montjuïc? Or to the beach?' (Barcelona's got everything: beautiful buildings, good restaurants, the sea.)

'Yes,' said Simon. He wasn't listening to me at all.

'You're not listening to me at all!' I said.

'Sorry?' he said, looking back at me.

'I said "You're not listening to me at all".'

'OK, OK, sorry. It's just, well, I've got a lot that I have to think about.' He looked strange.

'Do you want to do something together this morning or not?' I asked.

'No. No, I don't . . .'

At that moment Adriana walked over to our table. 'Morning!' she said happily. 'It's a beautiful day. What are you two going to do today?'

'I don't know,' I said. I was watching Simon. He was smiling at Adriana.

'Well, look,' she said to me. 'We've got lots of free time. Let's go to the beach or something.'

'Yes, that's a great idea.' I was pleased. It was going to be a good day after all, I thought. But I didn't know what was going to happen then, did I?

Chapter 3 *A newspaper, a beach*

While I was waiting for Adriana in the hotel reception area I sat down at a table. There were newspapers on the table. Most of them were in Spanish or Catalan, but there was one from Britain. I began to read it. There was a story about a painting.

Thieves Steal Picture from Gallery

The Gardener

Two nights ago some men got into the Tate Gallery in London. They took a painting called *The Gardener* by the French painter Cézanne.

'It's one of our most famous pictures,' said gallery director Delia Hitchin. 'Everyone loves it. *The Gardener* is a beautiful picture. It is a good example of Cézanne's work.'

The thieves got in through a window at the back of the building. Nobody heard them. Nobody saw them. They cut the painting from its frame.

'This painting is really important,' says Ms Hitchin. 'We want it back. Please, if you know anything at all call us or the police.'

The Gardener is 65.4 x 54 centimetres. It is worth about two million pounds.

I looked up. Frank Shepherd was standing next to my chair. He was looking at the newspaper too.

'That's an interesting story,' he said.

'What story?'

'About the painting.'

'The thieves were very good,' I said. 'Nobody saw them in the gallery. Nobody heard them.'

'Yes. That's good all right,' Frank said. 'Oh, by the way, about your double bass.'

'Yes?' I said.

'I talked to the police here. A man called Portillo.'

'And?' I asked.

'He's going to try and find it,' Frank said.

'How?' I said. I wanted my double bass back.

'I don't know. I'm not a policeman. He's going to talk to the drivers of the truck, I think. And he's going to talk to the French police.'

At that moment we heard a voice.

'Frank!' somebody shouted. 'Frank Shepherd! I want to talk to you.'

I looked round. Candida Ashley-Morton, the leader of the double basses, was walking towards us.

'Excuse me!' said Frank. He walked up to Candida and the two of them went towards the hotel bar. Candida was talking quickly. Was she angry? I couldn't hear the conversation. They went into the bar.

The lift doors opened and Adriana got out with some of the other orchestra players.

Somebody was shouting in the hotel bar. It was Candida Ashley-Morton. She was shouting at Frank. There was a short silence. Then he shouted back. Everybody stood and listened.

'Come on,' Adriana said to us. 'It's their problem, not ours. Let's go to the beach and have some fun!'

If you haven't been to Barcelona, you must go. The city feels good and there's lots to do. One of the most famous areas of the city is a big street called *Les Rambles* – or the Ramblas in English. People walk in the middle of this street. Cars go on the sides. Tourists walk up and down it. It has trees and cafés, street musicians and street actors. People sell newspapers and flowers and birds in cages. They try and sell you things or paint your picture. It's always full of life, always full of people.

About twenty of us left the hotel that morning. We walked down the Ramblas. We were talking and laughing. At the bottom of the long street we walked past the boats and the restaurants and then we came to the beach.

It was a beautiful day. The sun was already high in the sky. There were a lot of people lying on the sand. Some of the orchestra ran to the sea and swam. Some began to play football on the beach. Adriana and I sat and watched. We put on our sunglasses and smiled at each other.

'Wow!' she said. 'This is fantastic! This is the life!'

She was right. It was a fantastic day. But we didn't know, then, about the future. The future wasn't fantastic at all.

Chapter 4 *The concert*

Concerts start late in Spain. It was half past nine and the theatre still wasn't full. My face was red because of the day's sun and it was very hot in the theatre.

At five to ten we walked on to the theatre stage and sat down. The audience stopped talking. Our conductor, Philip Worth, walked on to the stage at ten o'clock. He lifted his arms and we started to play a piece of music called 'In the South' by the English composer Edward Elgar. I looked at all the people in the audience. Simon was near the front. He smiled at me. I was playing very well. I was really happy – except for Simon's poor hand, of course.

After 'In the South' we played a guitar concerto by the Spanish composer Rodrigo. The guitarist was a young Catalan player. She was very good and everybody loved her. Then there was a break of twenty minutes before the second half of the concert. The orchestra went into a room behind the stage. We drank some water. Simon came in.

'That was great,' he said. 'You're playing very well.'

'Thanks,' I said. I was very happy. 'It's because of your instrument. It's because of you.'

'Don't say that,' he laughed.

'Why?' I asked him.

'It's not true.' For a minute he didn't look happy.

'Sorry,' I said.

He smiled at me. 'I'm going to sit at the back of the theatre for the second half,' he told me. 'OK?'

'Why?' I asked.

'To hear a different sound,' he answered. 'To hear you from the back of the theatre.'

'Oh, right. I understand.' Except I didn't really understand. Then he kissed my hand and I felt happy. Simon wasn't always nice to me.

'See you later,' I said.

We played Rachmaninov's Third Symphony after the break. It is difficult music, but I think we played it well. The audience were very happy, anyway.

I left the stage with Simon's double bass. I put it into its big white case and closed it. Then I looked for Simon, but he wasn't in the theatre. I went to the room behind the stage. Many of the orchestra players were there. They were talking happily. I waited for Simon. But he didn't come.

'Have you seen Simon?' I asked Adriana.

15

'Me? No. Why?' She was a bit red in the face. I told you. It was a very hot night.

'I can't find him,' I said, looking at her. 'He was at the front of the theatre for the first half. Then he went to the back. Now he isn't there.'

'He's probably at the hotel.'

'I hope so,' I told her.

'And another thing,' she said. 'Where's Frank?'

'Isn't he here?' I asked.

'I don't think so,' she said. 'I can't see him, anyway.'

I left the theatre with her. We talked about the concert. She said that everybody loved it. Yes, I agreed, it was really good.

We walked along the Ramblas. There were people out with their friends. Men and women. Boyfriends and girlfriends. Children. It was a lovely night. There was a man with a guitar. A woman was dancing to his music. People sat in the open-air cafés and drank beer and wine.

'It's a bit late for children,' I said.

'Not here,' Adriana said. This was her third time in Barcelona. 'Here everybody goes to bed very late.'

'Well, I can't understand it,' I answered. 'I'm very tired. I want to go to sleep.'

Ten minutes later we got to our hotel.

I didn't say goodnight to Simon. I couldn't find him.

'Do you want a drink?' Adriana asked.

'No thanks. I really am very tired.'

'OK,' she said, 'see you tomorrow morning.'

I got into the lift and went up to my floor. I thought about the concert. I thought I played well.

When I got to my room I went to the telephone. I tried

a number. No answer. I put the telephone down. I thought something was wrong. I wasn't happy. Simon wasn't with me. My lovely double bass wasn't with me.

'Oh well,' I thought. 'Maybe tomorrow will be better.'

Some people think the double bass is a funny instrument. They say it just goes *plonk plonk*, but it's not true. Double basses are wonderful. They look lovely and they have a warm sound – like a friend. They are different from other instruments, too. I mean, one violin looks a lot like another violin. Cellos all look the same too. (Well, maybe they're different colours, but most people think they look the same.) So do trumpets. But not double basses. Some are tall and thin, some are short and fat. Each one is a different person. Each one has its own sound.

My double bass is a dark rich brown. It's very old. It looks really beautiful. If you play it well it makes a special sound. And it is worth a lot of money. I love it more than anything else. It's a Panormo. Made in 1798. My parents bought it for me.

'What am I going to do without my beautiful Panormo?' I thought. 'And where is Simon? What is happening to me?'

I was very tired. I fell asleep.

Chapter 5 *Screams in the night*

I was asleep, but my head was full of pictures and stories. I was dreaming about double basses and violinists and parties on the beach. Simon was in my dream. Our conductor was in it. So was my old teacher, playing a double bass on the sand. Then I heard a different sound. Somebody was shouting. No, it was worse than that. Somebody was screaming, screaming very loudly. I opened my eyes. I woke up. It was five o'clock in the morning.

Somebody screamed again. And again. And again. This time I wasn't dreaming.

I got out of bed. I put on a T-shirt and some jeans and went out of my room. Doors were opening on the left and the right. Adriana came out of her room. She ran up to me. She was half asleep, still in her night-dress. 'What is it?' she asked sleepily. 'What's going on?'

'I don't know,' I answered.

Martin Audley (a trumpet player) came up to us.

'Who screamed?' he asked.

'Nobody knows,' I told him. 'But it sounded terrible.'

There was another scream. It came from outside.

We ran back into my room and looked out of the window, down at the street. There was a police car there, some people, more and more people. And something else.

'Come on,' I said. We got the lift to the ground floor. When it stopped we ran out of the hotel and pushed to the front of all the people.

Marilyn Whittle, the harp player, was already there. Her face was white and her eyes were large and round.

'Look! Look!' she said. She was pointing in front of her. She screamed again.

We looked. She was pointing at the person at her feet. It was Frank Shepherd. His mouth was open. There was blood all over his head.

Martin spoke first. 'My God!' he said. 'He's dead!'

For a few minutes nobody did anything. It was like a moment from a bad film. I looked around me. Candida Ashley-Morton was there. Her face was white.

'Oh, oh, oh no,' she was saying, and then she turned and walked back into the hotel.

We knew that we couldn't sleep. We didn't know what to do. But the hotel manager was a nice person. He opened the bar – at half past five in the morning. We sat there. We were all asking the same questions. What happened? How did Frank die? Did he fall from his room?

We heard another police car. A man came into the bar. We stopped talking.

'Good morning,' he said. 'My name is Portillo, Inspector Portillo.' His voice was cold. So were his eyes. But I also thought, 'He's very good-looking with his dark hair and those eyes'. Then I felt bad because of Frank.

'Now, please listen everybody,' the policeman said. 'Mr Shepherd is dead. We can't change that. So go to bed. We'll talk tomorrow – well, I mean later today.' His English was very good.

Outside it was getting light. I was lying on my bed, thinking about Frank. I was trying not to see the blood and his eyes, open and dead. I was trying not to, but I couldn't stop. Someone knocked on my door. I got up and opened it. It was Simon.

'Hello,' he said.

'Hi. Isn't it terrible?'

'Yes,' he said. 'Poor Frank.'

'Where were you?' I asked. 'After the concert? Where were you last night?'

'I went to a bar,' he said.

'Why?' I asked.

'Why? Why? What a stupid question. For a drink.'

'What did you do then?' I asked.

'Questions, questions! Why all these questions?' His voice was different now.

'What did you do then?' I asked again.

'I went to another bar.' He wasn't smiling now.

'Why didn't you tell me?' I said. 'I needed you.' I was thinking of Frank's body again. 'You didn't come to my room when you got back.'

'Is that a question or a statement?'

'I don't know. Come on, Simon, where were you?' I didn't want to ask all these questions but I couldn't help it.

'All right. All right,' he shouted. 'Look, I went to a few bars, OK? I had a lot to drink. A lot. I walked back to the hotel very late. About three in the morning. When I got here I went up to my room quickly. I wasn't feeling very well, you see. All those drinks . . .'

'Were you with someone else?'

'Haven't you listened to me?' Now he was really angry. I didn't understand it.

'Oh Simon, I'm sorry,' I said. 'I'm being stupid. It's just, well, you know . . .'

'Yes,' he said. He was quieter now. 'It's been a difficult night, a difficult morning.' He smiled at me. He kissed me. But there was something wrong. Something wasn't quite right.

'I'm going to go back to my room,' he said. 'I need a shower. See you later.' He walked out of the room without another word.

I looked at the closed door. I thought about his words, about his answers to my questions. And then I thought, 'Why isn't he telling me the truth?'

Chapter 6 *Inspector Portillo*

Three and a half hours later on that same day I sat down with Inspector Portillo in the hotel dining room.

'Good morning, Miss Wade,' he said.

'Good morning,' I answered. I was a bit afraid. Why did he want to see me? Why were the police talking to everybody?

'I know about you,' he said.

'You do?' I asked.

'Yes. You're the player with the double bass.'

'Without the double bass,' I said.

'Yes,' he laughed. 'But we're looking for it.'

'Will you find it?' I asked.

'I hope so.'

'He isn't cold,' I thought. 'He's very nice. I like him.'

Then, suddenly, he changed. 'Now I have some questions for you.'

'Why?' I asked.

'That is not a very intelligent question,' he said. 'Someone has died. We always ask questions.'

'So you think I'm stupid, do you?' I was angry and very, very tired.

'No, of course not. I am very sorry,' he said. I looked into his face. He really *was* sorry.

'Forget it!' I said. 'I'm just tired.'

'Yes, so am I,' he smiled. 'Now, can I ask you some questions?'

'Yes,' I answered unhappily.

'Where were you last night?' he said suddenly.

'I was at the concert,' I replied.

'Yes, yes. Of course. And after the concert?'

'I came back to the hotel.'

'Who with?' said Inspector Portillo.

'With Adriana Fox. We walked up the Ramblas together.'

'OK,' Portillo said. 'You got back to the hotel. And then?'

'And then I went to bed,' I explained.

'Just you?' he asked with a smile.

'What? What do you mean?' I said.

'Are you married?' he asked. 'Do you have a boyfriend?'

'I'm not married. But I've got a boyfriend,' I said. 'I think.'

'Who is he?' Inspector Portillo asked.

'Do you have to know?' I asked. 'Is it important?'

'I'll ask you a different question,' he said. His voice was cold again. I didn't understand why. 'Do you have a boyfriend in the orchestra?'

'That's a very personal question,' I said.

'Death is very personal,' he said, very quietly.

'Yes. Sorry,' I said. I suddenly saw Frank's body again.

'So?' he asked.

'What?' I said.

'What's the answer? Do you have a boyfriend in the orchestra?'

'Yes,' I said.

'Who is that?'

'Simon Hunt,' I told him.

'And did he, did you spend the night together?'

'Well no, we didn't,' I said. I wasn't enjoying this.

'I see.' He put his pen in his mouth. He didn't say anything for a moment. Then he looked into my eyes. 'All right,' he said. 'That's all.'

'You aren't going to ask me any more questions?' I said, 'I can go?'

'Yes. For now. But don't go far. Nobody in the orchestra must leave Barcelona. Stay near the hotel.'

'Of course.'

'I'll talk to you again,' he said. He was smiling again. 'All right?'

'Oh yes,' I said. 'Good.' But I didn't feel good at all.

Chapter 7   *Secrets*

'It's going to be strange without Frank,' Adriana said.

'Yes,' I agreed. 'Very strange.'

We were sitting in a café. Adriana was drinking an orange juice and I was drinking my third cup of coffee. We both felt very sad.

'You've been in the orchestra for two months,' Adriana said. 'I've been in it for three years. Frank was like a father to me. He was a nice man.'

'Yes,' I said. We talked about Frank. We didn't talk about his body in the street, but I remembered everything. I remembered the screams. I remembered the people in the street, people running in the hotel, Martin, Candida, Adriana. Pictures, pictures. In my head. I sat up. Some coffee fell on to my T-shirt. Something in the pictures was wrong.

'Are you OK?' Adriana asked.

'Yes. No.' I needed time to think. I didn't want questions from Adriana.

'Listen, Penny . . . ' she began.

'Yes?' I said.

'Oh, nothing,' she replied. Then she looked up at someone behind me. I turned round.

'Simon!' I said. 'Hello. Where have you been?'

'Oh, here and there,' he replied. 'I was talking to some of the orchestra players. About Frank, of course.'

'Of course,' I said. 'Do you want to sit down?'

'Sure.' Adriana smiled at him. He smiled back. It was a special smile. They had a secret. Just the two of them. Something that I did not know. That nobody knew. I turned away.

Simon asked for a beer. When it came he drank it very quickly.

'What do you think's going to happen?' Adriana asked.

'About what?' Simon said.

'About our concerts – tomorrow here in Barcelona, then Madrid, Bilbao,' Adriana said.

'What do you mean?' Simon asked.

'Well,' my friend explained. 'Frank's dead. He was our orchestra manager. He's been with the orchestra for twenty years. How can we play tomorrow night without him?'

'But it's an important concert tomorrow night,' I said. 'More than two thousand people are coming.'

'Yes, that's a problem,' said a voice next to me. I looked up. Martin Audley was standing there.

'Martin,' said Adriana. She looked uncomfortable. 'What are you doing here?'

'I'm looking for Penny, actually,' Martin told her.

'Me?' I said.

'Yes,' Martin said. 'Inspector Portillo wants to speak to you again.'

'When?' I asked.

'Now. This minute.'

'I'll go then.' I looked at Simon. He wasn't smiling at all now.

I got up and walked away from the table. I looked back. Martin was sitting with them now. The sun was hot but I began to run. I was running away from the picture in my head. The picture of last night in the hotel.

But I couldn't stop the picture. I was back in the hotel, back in my room. I heard the screams. I ran out of my room. Other people ran out of their rooms. Other players.

Adriana, for example. Her room was six doors down from mine. I could see her, but now I remembered something else. She came from her room, but she wasn't the only one there. Somebody was in the room with her. I saw him in the dark, but I couldn't see him well. Who was it?

I thought of Adriana in the café. Smiling at Simon. Was that their secret?

I ran into the hotel. Inspector Portillo was waiting for me.

'I am very sorry,' he started. 'But I have got some more questions.'

'So have I,' I said. 'Did somebody kill Frank?'

'Maybe.' He smiled a secret smile.

'What do you mean by "maybe"? Have you found Frank's killer? What do you know?' I asked.

'Miss Wade,' he said. 'There's something the police here always do, something we have always done.'

'What's that?' I asked, stupidly.

'Well, *we* ask the questions, *you* give the answers.' I think he was laughing at me. 'Is that all right with you?' he asked.

I didn't say anything.

'That means yes, I think. Now Mr Simon Hunt is your boyfriend, you said?' asked the inspector.

'Yes,' I answered.

'And he plays the double bass too, I believe?'

'Yes,' I said.

'Is he a good bass player?'

'Oh yes,' I said immediately. 'He's better than me. He's the number two. The second best in the whole orchestra.'

'Yes,' the inspector said. 'Somebody told me that.'

'Why are we talking about Simon?' I asked, but he didn't answer me. He just looked and looked. 'Sorry,' I said, 'I remember. *You* ask the questions.'

'You are a quick learner Miss Wade.' Now I was sure. He was laughing at me. 'Mr Hunt didn't play in the concert last night, did he?' he said suddenly.

'No,' I told him. 'I played in his place. He lent me his double bass. Because I haven't got mine with me.'

'Yes,' he said. 'I haven't forgotten.'

'Sorry, of course not,' I said. Was he angry with me?

'Did Simon Hunt go to the concert?' he asked.

'Oh yes. He was at the front,' I told him. I was thinking of Simon's handsome face.

'Was he at the front all the time?' Inspector Portillo said.

'No. In the second half he sat at the back.'

'Did you see him at the back?' His voice was cold again.

'Yes. I mean, no.' I wasn't sure. 'It's a big theatre.'

'And after the concert?' the inspector asked. 'What did Mr Hunt do then?'

'He went to a bar – well, he went to three or four bars I think,' I told him.

'Did you see him at the hotel?'

'No . . . look, why are you asking all these questions about Simon? You should ask me about Candida,' I said.

'Candida?' he said.

'Yes, Candida Ashley-Morton,' I said. 'The leader of the double basses.'

'What about her?'

'I think . . . I think that perhaps she killed Frank,' I said. 'Well, perhaps she didn't kill him, but she knows something. I'm sure.'

29

'Why do you say that?' he asked.

'Well, because I heard something. She was very angry with him yesterday morning.' I told Inspector Portillo about the conversation between Candida and Frank in the hotel bar.

When I finished he sat back in his chair.

'That is most interesting, Miss Wade,' he said. 'Most interesting.'

'Well, yes. So you must talk to them.'

'Thank you,' said the police inspector. 'I will think about it. And Penny – I mean, Miss Wade – I am sorry about all the questions.'

I got up and walked out of the room. Candida Ashley-Morton. Yes. Perhaps she killed Frank. Did the inspector believe that? Did I? What was the truth?

Twenty-four hours later I had the answer.

Chapter 8   *A restaurant, a fight*

That evening some of us went to a restaurant near the Ramblas. Simon didn't come with us.

'I have to see some people. I'll come back to the hotel later,' he told me. I was sitting next to Martin. I like Martin. He's been in the orchestra for about six years.

Adriana was at the other side of the table. Sometimes she smiled at me and I smiled back. But all the time I was thinking, 'Was that Simon in her room? Is she trying to be my friend and Simon's lover at the same time?' He wasn't in his room last night. Somebody was in hers.

'Oh no,' I thought. 'Why is life so difficult?'

We finished our supper and paid the bill. Then we walked back up the Ramblas.

Adriana came up to me. 'Are you OK?' she said. We were walking past a café.

'Now, now,' I thought. 'Now is a good time for the question – the question I want to ask her.'

But at that moment we heard English voices. We turned round. Candida Ashley-Morton was sitting at one of the tables. Marilyn Whittle, the harp player, was standing up. She was shouting at Candida. People were watching them.

'Was it you?' she was shouting. 'Did you push him out of the window?'

'No, of course, I didn't,' Candida said quietly. 'Don't be stupid.'

'I think you did,' the harp player said. 'You killed him. Because he didn't love you.'

'What are you talking about?' Candida's face was white.

'You loved him, didn't you?' Marilyn said. Her face was all red.

Candida looked at the ground. She didn't say anything.

'Didn't you?' screamed Marilyn. 'You were in love with him!'

'All right. It's true,' Candida said. 'Frank and I were lovers. There, are you happy?'

'That's why you killed him!' Marilyn shouted.

'What are you talking about?' Candida said again. Her voice sounded tired.

'You killed him because he didn't love you anymore,' Marilyn told her.

'Please stop. Everyone's listening.'

'Everybody's listening?' she said. 'So what? Let them listen. I'll tell them a story. About a man called Frank Shepherd. I loved him too, you know.'

'Yes,' Candida said quietly. 'He told me.'

'That's not true!' the harp player shouted back. 'He didn't tell you. He didn't love you. He loved me. More than you. He loved me.'

'Stop it, Marilyn,' Candida said. 'Go back to the hotel. Go back to your room. You need some sleep.'

'Sleep? I can't sleep. Frank's dead. How can I sleep? With a killer in the next room.'

'Now listen, Marilyn, you must stop this.'

'I won't stop it. You're a killer, a killer, a dirty killer. You pushed him out of that window because he loved me.

Me. He loved me.' Marilyn was shouting louder and louder. She had a terrible look in her eyes. Everybody on the street stopped to watch. I didn't know what to do.

Adriana walked over to the harp player. 'Stop it!' she said to her. 'Stop it!' And she hit Marilyn hard in the face.

Marilyn opened her mouth to say something. Then she closed it and ran out of the café.

'Go after her, Martin,' Adriana said, and Martin followed the unhappy harp player into the night.

'I'm sorry about that,' Candida said, 'I'm sorry. It's not true, of course. Really. It's not true.' She was crying now.

'Let's talk about it tomorrow,' Adriana said. She put her arm around Candida and we walked away, up the Ramblas, towards our hotel.

I spent that night with Simon. He arrived an hour after we did. He was nice to me. He got into bed next to me, and kissed my eyes. He talked of love and I wanted to believe him. He had a bottle of champagne with him.

But I wasn't happy. I loved Simon, but I didn't feel good about it. He was strange towards me. Sometimes he said things and did things which I didn't understand. But he tried to love me, I think. He tried to love me that night, perhaps because he knew something that I didn't know. He knew that it was our last night together.

When I woke up he was gone.

Chapter 9   *Two men, a truck, and a double bass*

I couldn't find Simon after breakfast. I couldn't find him anywhere in the hotel.

The morning passed very slowly. The orchestra players talked to each other, but not much. A few of us went for a walk, but we didn't go far. We were all waiting.

After lunch we all went back to the hotel dining room. Well, nearly all of us.

Philip Worth, our conductor, walked into the room. Inspector Portillo was with him.

'Good afternoon, everybody,' said our conductor. Everybody stopped talking.

'Now as you know, Inspector Portillo asked you all questions yesterday. Now he has some answers. Jorge.'

Jorge? Inspector Jorge Portillo. That was the inspector's name? I liked it.

'Thank you, *Maestro*,' said Inspector Portillo. 'At this moment we don't know everything. We have to talk to some more people. But I will tell you my idea of the story. I think it is the real story, but . . .' he looked around the room, 'some things are still not clear.' He looked at me and smiled.

'You all came to Barcelona by air,' he started. 'Because it's quicker than a coach. But the big instruments came in the BSO truck with two drivers. The double basses were in that truck, of course. They drove to Dover and put the truck on the boat. Then they drove through France towards Spain.

After twelve hours the truck drivers were tired. They stopped at a café by the side of the road. Near Toulouse in France. They went into the café and had a cup of coffee and something to eat. Then a car arrived. A big car, I think. It went up to the truck. Two men got out – well, we think it was two. They went to the truck. They opened it – I'm sure they had the key. Then they saw *it* and they smiled.'

'What? What did they see?' Marilyn asked.

'The double bass of Miss Penny Wade,' said the inspector.

'What? What did they see?' I asked.

'They saw your double bass, Miss Wade.'

'Why my double bass?' I didn't understand what he was talking about. 'They weren't looking for it, were they?'

'Oh yes,' Inspector Portillo said. 'That's what they were looking for.'

'But who? Why? How did they know it was my double bass?' I asked.

'I think somebody wrote your name on the case. The two men saw it and they took it from the truck.'

'I don't understand,' Adriana said. 'Why did they take Penny's double bass?'

'Well, I don't think they wanted Miss Wade's instrument,' the inspector said. 'They wanted the case.'

'The case?' Martin said. 'Why did they want the case?'

'Well, actually,' Inspector Portillo said. 'They didn't want the case. They wanted something in the case.'

'What? What was it?' I couldn't wait any longer.

'A picture.'

'A picture? What kind of a picture?' Adriana asked.

'It was a painting. By the French artist Cézanne. It's called "The Gardener". Somebody took it from the Tate Gallery in London . . .'

'Oh yes,' I shouted. 'I read about it in the paper. It's worth two million pounds. Wow!'

'Thank you Miss Wade,' said Inspector Portillo. I wasn't sure, but I think he was smiling at me again. I smiled back. 'So somebody took the painting from the Tate Gallery. And then somebody – it wasn't the same person, of course – put it in Miss Wade's double bass case.'

'Why didn't they take the picture and leave the double bass?' I asked.

'I don't know. Perhaps they didn't have time. Perhaps some people came out of the café. But they closed the truck and drove away with Miss Wade's bass in its big white case.'

'Inspector,' Martin said. 'You say "I think", "perhaps", "I don't know". What do you *know*? Is this story true?'

'That's a good question,' Inspector Portillo replied.

'Yes, but what's the answer?' Martin said.

'The answer is this. Miss Wade's double bass was in the truck when it left Barston. It wasn't in the truck when it got to Barcelona. The truck stopped for a long time only once. And a French driver saw two men with something big and white there. Something like a double bass case.'

'How do you know that?' Adriana asked.

'The French police told us,' the inspector said.

'Where's my double bass now?' I asked.

'I'm sorry, Miss Wade,' said Inspector Portillo.

'But I don't know.' He liked me, I thought. He really was sorry.

'What about the painting?' Martin asked.

'That's safe,' Inspector Portillo said. 'The French police found it this morning in Paris.'

'Excuse me!' Adriana said.

'Yes?' said Inspector Portillo.

'You said Frank died because of the truck. But how? Why? What do you mean? Did he die because of the painting? Did he put the painting in Penny's double bass case, or what?'

'Those are all good questions,' Inspector Portillo replied. 'They were our questions too. At first we didn't understand why Mr Shepherd died. Did he fall out of that window? Did he jump? Did somebody push him? Did he have problems? With a lover? A friend? Was there an argument?'

I looked over at Candida Ashley-Morton. Her head was in her hands. She was crying, I think. Perhaps she really did do it. Inspector Portillo was still speaking.

'But then we talked to the hotel people. We looked at the rooms. And immediately we had a problem.'

'What problem?' Martin asked.

'The window in Mr Shepherd's room was closed,' Inspector Portillo said.

'He didn't like open windows,' Candida said quietly.

'That is correct.' Inspector Portillo looked at Candida when he said this. 'And a man cannot jump out of a closed window.'

'What are you saying?' Martin asked.

'I am saying that Frank Shepherd didn't jump out of the window of his room. He fell from a different room.'

There was silence in the hotel dining room now – complete silence.

'That was difficult for us,' the inspector said. 'Whose room was it? We didn't know. But then one of my men looked at everything on the hotel computer. He looked at the telephone calls. Then he saw it. Somebody telephoned the police in London last night. What was the room number? He looked on the computer. It was Frank Shepherd's room. Frank Shepherd telephoned London.'

'Frank called the police in London?' Marilyn asked. 'Why?'

'We asked the police in London the same question. "Why did Frank Shepherd telephone you?" They told us.'

'Wait a minute,' Martin said. 'I thought Frank fell from somebody else's window. But you said he telephoned from his room.'

'You are quite correct,' the inspector said. 'He telephoned from his room. Then he went to somebody else's room.'

'Whose?' Candida asked. 'Do you know what happened to Frank. Do you know the name of his killer?'

'Oh yes, we know. We know.' And suddenly I knew too.

Chapter 10 *Why did you do it?*

Sometimes, now, I still can't believe what happened in Barcelona. I don't know the whole story, of course, but I know most of it.

Simon did not stay for the second half of the concert in the theatre in Barcelona that night. 'No problem,' he thought, 'Penny saw me at the concert. The orchestra saw me. Penny thinks I'm sitting at the back.' Poor Simon.

Simon went to a bar to meet someone. But Frank was also in the bar. Frank needed a drink. He needed to think about his problems. You see Frank loved Candida. But then Marilyn decided that she loved Frank too. She sent him letters, gave him things, talked to him, followed him everywhere. Frank didn't like Marilyn following him. He needed a drink.

Simon didn't see Frank. Frank didn't see Simon either, at first. But the barman saw Frank – and later he saw a picture of Frank on the television – so he rang the police.

A tall Frenchman came into the bar with a black bag. Perhaps that's when Frank looked up and saw Simon, but he didn't speak to him. Frank knew that something wasn't right.

'Thank you *Monsieur* Hunt,' the Frenchman said. 'We have got the picture. My friend is very happy.' He opened his bag. He gave Simon a large brown envelope. Frank was listening.

'All this, just for a Cézanne painting,' Simon laughed.

Frank probably remembered the article in the newspaper. The Frenchman walked out of the bar. Simon looked into the envelope. There was money in it. A lot of money. Frank saw it too. It was money for 'The Gardener' by Cézanne, of course. Frank didn't know the whole story then, but we know now: a rich man in France wanted it for his secret collection of art. Something else Frank didn't know. Simon's cousin worked at the Tate Gallery as a security guard. She took the painting from the gallery. She gave it to Simon and he put it in my double bass case. Nobody looks for a painting in a double bass case in an orchestra truck!

Simon went back to the hotel. Frank went to his own room first and made that phone call to London. Then he went to Simon's room. Perhaps he wanted to ask him, 'Why? Why did you do it?' Perhaps he wanted to tell him to run. I don't know. But it wasn't a good idea to go to Simon's room. Simon's window was open. Frank fell five floors to the ground.

The police found Simon at Barcelona airport. He went there after his night with me.

*   *   *

The policeman walked through the police station. I followed him. It was very hot in the building.

We got to a door. The policeman unlocked the door.

There was a different policeman in the room. And Simon.

'Hello,' Simon said. He looked terrible.

'Hello,' I said quietly. 'How are you?'

'What do you think?' he said. It wasn't a real question.

'Oh Simon, did you really kill Frank?' I asked him.

42

'Yes. No. He was angry. He fell. Well, I pushed him.'

'Why?' I asked. I couldn't believe this.

'He saw me in the bar,' Simon said in an unfriendly voice. 'He saw me with the Frenchman. He knew about "The Gardener".'

'Why?' I shouted. 'Why did you do it?' I was very angry.

'Why did I do it? Money, of course. I wanted more money.'

'And why didn't you run?' I asked.

'I did. After Frank "fell", I left the hotel. But then I

thought. "Nobody knows. It was an accident. That's what people will say." But I didn't know about his telephone call. I didn't know that the police could see where his fingers were, his fingerprints on the window of my room.'

We sat in that room for a few more minutes. We didn't look at each other.

'What's going to happen to you?' I asked.

'What do you think? I'm going to be in prison for a long time, I expect.'

'Poor Simon.'

'Oh, be quiet. Go away. Go away. I don't want you in this room. I don't want anybody here with me. I don't want to see you again. Ever. Just get out.'

I wanted to stay. Simon was not a good person, but I loved him. Well, I loved him once upon a time.

'Simon,' I said. 'Simon I . . .' but I didn't have any words in my head. Simon looked at the floor. The Spanish policeman looked out of the window. I left the room.

When I walked out of the police station I didn't look back.

Chapter 11 *One more question*

We left Barcelona. I was very unhappy. I thought about Simon in prison. We played concerts in Madrid and Bilbao. We didn't play very well, of course, but we played.

On our last night in Bilbao, Adriana and I went out after the concert.

'Are you going to be all right?' Adriana said. 'You've had a terrible time.'

We were walking by the Río Nervión, Bilbao's big, black river.

'Adriana,' I said. 'Can I ask you something?'

'Yes, of course.'

'Do you – did you like Simon before?'

'Well, I liked him.'

'Were you very good friends?'

'What? What are you asking? Like lovers?' Adriana asked.

'No. Yes. No. I don't know.' Why did I start this, I thought.

'Of course he wasn't my lover,' she laughed. 'Why did you think that?'

'I didn't, really. It's just, well, you had a secret.'

'Ah. That . . . ' She stopped and looked at me.

'You did have a secret, didn't you?' I asked.

'Yes, yes we did.' She was silent for a minute. I waited. 'Simon saw us, you see. He saw me with Martin.'

'Martin!' Now I was really surprised.

'Yes. We've been together for three months. But we didn't want to tell anyone.'

'So the night Simon killed Frank?' I asked. 'Somebody was in your room . . .'

'You thought it was Simon! Oh, Penny!'

'I'm sorry,' I said.

'It was Martin, of course, you silly thing.' She laughed.

'I'm sorry,' I said again.

'Now listen to me,' said Adriana. 'Don't feel sorry, don't think about Simon. Start your life again. Start thinking of the future.'

That's when I heard it. Music. Someone was playing a guitar. Somebody else was playing a violin. But that wasn't all. There was another instrument too.

'Adriana!' I shouted. 'Listen!'

'What?'

'That sound. I know that sound. Come on.'

We ran by the side of the river. We ran to the music. The players in the street were very good. We stood there, listening to the guitar and the violin. And a double bass. A beautiful double bass with a special sound. A Panormo. Made in 1798. It was my double bass.

'Hey,' I said. 'That's my double bass.'

'No, it isn't,' said the double bass player.

'All right,' I said, 'Where did you get it?'

'Well, I . . . er . . . I . . . it's mine,' he said again.

'That's not true,' Adriana said. 'It's not your double bass and you know it!'

The double bass player was not sure what to do. He didn't look very happy. He knew that something was wrong.

'All right,' he said. 'All right. A man sold it to me. Very cheap. In the street. It wasn't right. I know. But I don't like it anyway. The sound is all wrong. You give me some money and you can have it.'

Finally we gave him some money, but not much. I went to the bass player and took the lovely instrument. It was dirty and there were some black lines on the wood. But I loved it anyway. I was very happy. I put my arms around it.

'Come on,' I said to it. 'Let's go home.'

At that moment a car came round the corner and stopped. Two policemen got out. I didn't know the first one, but I knew the second.

'Ah,' he said. 'Hello Miss Wade. Penny.'

'Inspector Portillo,' I said. 'What are you doing here? You work in Barcelona.'

'That is true. I work in Barcelona.'

'So why are you here?'

'We ask the questions,' he said. He was laughing at me. 'You have found something, I see,' he said.

'Yes, it's my double bass. Isn't it fantastic!'

'It is good news, yes. You said it was a very good double bass. It looks nice. But I think its player is more beautiful.'

'Sorry?' I said.

'Why do you think I am in Bilbao, Penny Wade?' the inspector said. He *was* very good-looking.

'Come on, Penny,' Adriana said. 'It's time we went back to the hotel.'

'I will take you,' my inspector said. 'Your double bass can go in our car, I think. Come on. Then I want to ask Miss Wade a question.'

'More questions! I don't believe it.' I said.

'Only one,' he said. 'I've only got one more question.'

And he did ask me one more question. The most surprising question in the world. And my answer? 'I'll think about it.' And I have thought about it. Maybe there is a future after all. I'm going back to Spain tomorrow.

GRIPPING WAR STORIES

COLLECTED BY
TONY BRADMAN

Illustrated by Jon Riley

CORGI BOOKS

A CORGI BOOK: 978 0 552 56732 9

First published in Great Britain by Doubleday,
a division of Transworld Publishers Ltd

PRINTING HISTORY
Doubleday edition published 1998
Corgi edition published 1999

1 3 5 7 9 10 8 6 4 2

Set in 14/16 Bembo by Falcon Oast Graphic Art

Corgi Books are published by Transworld Publishers Ltd,
61-63 Uxbridge Road, Ealing, London W5 5SA,

Addresses for companies within The Random House Group Limited
can be found at: www.randomhouse.co.uk/offices.htm

The Random House Group Limited supports The Forest Stewardship
Council (FSC®), the leading international forest certification organisation.
Our books carrying the FSC label are printed on FSC® certified paper.
FSC is the only forest certification scheme endorsed by the leading
environmental organisations, including Greenpeace. Our
paper procurement policy can be found at
www.randomhouse.co.uk/environment

MIX
Paper from
responsible sources
FSC
www.fsc.org   FSC® C018072

Printed and bound in Great Britain by Clays Ltd, St Ives PLC

CONTENTS

DESERTER
by Anthony Masters

Eric gazed around him disbelievingly, his mouth dry and his heart pounding. The Falklands valley he had loved so much, with its unyielding grey rock, tussock grass and soft boggy ground, had been devastated, transformed into a man-made hell, a scrap-metal merchant's dream.

Bewildered geese fluttered over the debris of the battlefield, while cattle and sheep wandered aimlessly. Those were the lucky ones. Some were just carcasses, lying where they had been shot or blown apart by a mine.

Eric knew he shouldn't be here, that his parents had forbidden him to come anywhere near this dreadful

7

place. But Buster, the Laker family's beloved old sheepdog, had gone missing.

Guessing he had probably been terrified by the sound of last night's battle, Eric was determined to look for him. The artillery fire, the blasting of anti-aircraft guns and the clattering of helicopters was still in his own ears. But maybe Buster was just dutifully trying to herd up the family's scattered sheep.

Eric wished his parents hadn't been asked to take away some of the Argentinian wounded. The ground was too soft for field ambulances and there weren't enough four-wheel drives, so Mr and Mrs Laker were heading for Port Stanley with the tractor and trailer, having told Eric to stay in the farmhouse. But neither of them had noticed Buster had gone and Eric knew he had to find him before he, too, stepped on a mine.

Increasingly afraid for the old sheepdog, Eric wove his way through the devastation, while the geese seemed to hang listlessly in the steel-grey morning sky. Then he began to run cautiously through the abandoned military equipment that covered the valley floor. Cannon shells, field dressings, machine guns, rifles, ammunition cases and spent bullets were every-where amongst the craters, shell holes and shattered rock.

Eric shivered. He and his parents had sat through the night in an improvised bunker, listening to the Argentinian and British troops blowing each other apart. Now he could see the slit trenches of the Argentine positions and a number of rockets still lashed to long stout poles that protruded from the soft ground where sheep normally grazed. The sight was horrific.

A bitter wind blew a couple of helmets across the muddy ground towards him and freezing rain began to drum on the debris. Eric saw an open box of mortars, avoided a couple of camouflage nets, and then came across a boot. He didn't want to look any closer. Suppose it had part of a foot inside?

A couple of grubby white flags of surrender flapped in the beating wind and Eric hurried on, calling Buster, his voice thin and weak in the wilderness.

'The invasion's over,' his father had told him. 'There's been an Argentine surrender. You lock yourself in.'

But twelve-year-old Eric was determined to find Buster, whatever the dangers.

Eric knew that the Falkland Islands were among the bleakest and most desolate places on earth, but he had always loved his wilderness. He had lived on his parents' sheep farm all his life, except for an unhappy period when he had gone to boarding school in Buenos Aires on the Argentine mainland. Eric had hated the school – not because he was in Argentina, not because the work was hard and the lessons were in Spanish, but because he was desperately homesick for the rugged Falklands.

Eventually, Eric had become so unhappy in Buenos Aires that he had stopped eating and was flown home, to continue his education by radio on the Lakers' remote sheep farm.

On the edge of the battlefield, soaked and muddied almost beyond recognition, Eric noticed a Spanish Bible and was reminded of the young Argentine soldiers on the mountain last week. He and Buster had been moving the sheep along a twilit ridge when they had come across them. Some had been kneeling, while one lieutenant, wounded in the leg, had stood with a rosary in his hand. The soldiers had been lit by the flames of the gorse bushes they had set on fire to keep warm.

Eric had been as angry as any other Falklander when Argentina invaded the islands which had always been a British protectorate. The Argentines had announced they had come to reclaim territory which rightfully belonged to them, but the British had disagreed and their army had arrived to fight them off.

Eric had felt a sense of importance, of actually belonging to the United Kingdom, the far away country he had never seen. He wanted to be liberated and, judging by what Dad had said, he just had been. But at what cost? As he ran, he gazed around at the debris of war and wondered how many soldiers had died here.

Eric didn't care which side they were on; it was all

such a waste. He had never hated the Argentines, never called them 'Argies', as some of the Falklanders and most of the British did. After all, he had been to school with them. He knew the Argentines. He didn't know the British.

'Buster!' Eric yelled into the raw bitterness of the rising wind and rain. 'Where are you, Buster?' Suppose the dog was dead? Eric's eyes began to sting with tears.

He gazed down at the cove, the spume rising as the waves tore at the black rock. Terns wheeled over the tumult, but he could just make out the sound of barking above their plaintive cries.

Then, to his joy, he saw Buster down on the pebbles of Sea Wrack cove, running in and out of a cave entrance, his bark becoming an angry howl.

'I'm coming, boy,' he yelled into the darting wind. 'I'm coming, Buster.' But he knew there was no chance of the old sheepdog hearing or even seeing him, as mist rolled up out of the ferocious sea. Without even thinking about the mines, Eric began to run as hard as he could, thankful that he was wearing heavy boots, jeans and a thick anorak.

He arrived on the beach in a flurry of mud and rain, still calling Buster's name. But the dog seemed to have retreated into the cave mouth.

What was the matter with him? Eric wondered, his relief draining away. Was there a sheep in there or had

Buster been driven mad by the battle – just as some men must be? He could hear him barking faintly and paused. The caves were known as the Labyrinth, and they stretched for miles under the cliff. It would be all too easy to get lost in them. 'Folks have gone in and never come out,' his dad had warned him repeatedly.

What was he going to do? Eric called Buster over and over again, but his barking only seemed to get fainter.

Eric plunged into the darkness of the caves, listening intently for the sound of Buster's barking. Trying to remember the way, he kept reciting to himself, 'Left . . . left . . . left . . . right . . . left.' Soon he became confused. Hadn't it really been left, right, left? Or wasn't it left and then right?

Panic swept him and Eric found himself sweating, feverish, but determined to continue.

Soon the barking became much louder and, within seconds, illuminated by wan torchlight, Buster appeared, leaping up at something that was lying on a ledge.

Buster was still barking furiously.

Suddenly the beam shone directly into Eric's eyes, dazzling him. Someone was there. Someone different, alien. Terrified, he saw huge eyes that looked as if they were on stalks. The scream began in his throat and stuck there, vibrating inside him.

Then Eric realized what he was looking at and felt an utter fool. The man was wearing PNGs – passive night goggles – which were designed to intensify night images and were worn by British and Argentine soldiers alike.

The figure moved slightly, huddling away from Buster's still relentless barking, and Eric caught a glimpse of a light machine gun and the Argentine insignia on the torn and muddied combat jacket.

Trying not to panic, he placed a restraining hand on Buster's neck, reassuringly rubbing his fur, trying to calm him down but not succeeding. What was he going to do? Should he turn and run?

The soldier struggled to an upright position, putting the torch down on the rock and holding his machine gun in both hands.

'Water,' came the hoarse voice.

'I haven't got any. Are you hurt?'

The soldier didn't reply. Then, to his horror, Eric heard a click.

Had he taken off the safety catch on the machine gun? Was he going to kill them both? Then a sudden thought occurred to him. Why hadn't he shot Buster already?

Eric struggled to remember at least some of the Spanish he had learnt at the school in Buenos Aires, but the chill inside him had made his mind go blank. Eventually he managed, '*Te lastimaste?*' He repeated the phrase in English. 'Are you hurt?'

There was a long silence.

Then the hoarse voice replied, 'Yes.'

'*Soy un amigo*,' stuttered Eric. 'I'm a friend.' Well, he was hardly that but never mind, as long as he could persuade the soldier not to kill him. He felt a pounding in his temples, and a roaring in his ears.

Buster was growling softly now, as if he, too, knew of the terrible danger they were both in.

'Water,' repeated the soldier.

'I'll get some,' said Eric, backing off. 'I shan't be long.' Could this be his chance of escape?

The Argentine soldier dragged off his goggles. 'No,' he rasped. 'Don't move.'

Does he know the war's over? Eric wondered. Should he tell him? He decided to take the risk. 'Your army has surrendered.'

He felt the soldier's eyes on him.

'The Argentines have surrendered. The war's over.'

There was another long silence. Then the soldier muttered something and gave a grunt of pain.

Eric heard the click of a trigger. He shut his eyes and waited for the bullet to cut him down.

The soldier pulled the trigger again and Eric wondered if he had already been hit. He couldn't feel anything but perhaps he was already dying. He gasped for air.

There was a dry laugh and Eric opened his eyes. Immediately the rocky sides of the tunnel closed in on him and he staggered. The sense of relief was overwhelming and gradually the faintness passed. The soldier had been bluffing.

Or had he? He was now pointing the machine gun at Buster and Eric felt sick. 'Please don't,' he whispered, sure the soldier's finger was on the trigger now, that he was actually going to fire. 'Please,' he repeated as Buster growled.

Then he heard the sound of sobbing.

Eric gazed at his tormentor in bewilderment. The crying was desolate but also childish, and he knew the game was over.

'Empty,' the soldier muttered. He threw the gun down on the floor with a dull clatter but grabbed the torch.

'What's the matter?' Eric asked, but the sobbing continued and he was reminded of how he had cried so bitterly on his own in Buenos Aires for love of the Falklands. Was the soldier doing the same for Argentina?

'Give me the torch,' suggested Eric hesitantly. 'Buster and I can guide you out.'

The soldier shook his head, trying to stifle his sobs, and on impulse Eric lunged forward, knowing how stupid he was being but somehow unable to stop himself. He had to get back in charge again. This was *his* island. He didn't want interlopers, whether they were Argentine or British.

Eric felt a kick in the stomach and, surprised at the softness of the impact, he nevertheless lost his balance and fell back on to the hard rock.

He struggled to his feet again, grabbing Buster's collar as the old sheepdog began to bark furiously. Then he saw the stinking bundle of rags wrapped around the soldier's foot.

'You *are* hurt.' He suddenly realized that the Argentine soldier had contracted trench foot, a condition he had already seen in British soldiers, caused by spending endless days and nights on the soggy soil. Continuously wet and sore, his foot had eventually gone rotten. Eric shuddered.

Then he saw that the young soldier had dropped the torch and it was lying on the rocky floor, the beam still shining. They both rushed for it at the same time, but Eric got there first and ran back up the tunnel, Buster behind him, expecting pursuit but hearing none. He stopped, waiting.

On impulse, Eric returned, shining the torch directly on the soldier's face. He was young, probably no more than eighteen, with a pale, oval face, short dark hair and a growth of beard.

Buster resumed his growling as Eric asked, 'What's your name?'

'Paco.'

'*Soy un amigo*,' he repeated, wondering what he was going to do next. 'Eric.'

Paco shrugged.

'You come home with me. Have food and drink.' Eric moved a little nearer and flashed the torch into the soldier's frightened eyes.

'They shoot.'

'I told you. It's all over. You'll be a prisoner of war.'

'*Argentines* shoot me. I run.'

So you're a deserter, thought Eric. You think you'll be shot by your own people. He could sense Paco's fear and shame and wondered fleetingly what he would have done if he had been in his place.

For a moment Eric felt a surge of contempt. Running away – leaving his comrades – it was a dreadful thing to do. But he couldn't help feeling moved by Paco's plight. '*Soy un amigo*,' he repeated. 'I'm your friend. I'll help you.' Eric paused. 'I mean – you can't stay down here for ever. You'll die.'

Slowly Paco got to his feet. 'I come,' he said.

Flustered, unsure of himself, Eric began to walk into the darkness, the torch seeming weaker now.

A few minutes later, he knew that he was lost in the Labyrinth. He was sure he had taken a number of wrong turnings.

Paco was groaning behind him, and every so often he gave a little yelp of pain. Far from finding the way, Buster refused to go in front at all, determinedly

17

bringing up the rear as if to protect them from a surprise attack.

'*Estamos perdidos*?' asked Paco softly, and Eric stopped and turned round.

'Yes,' he said woodenly. 'We're lost.'

'Light.'

Eric looked down at the torch to see that its beam was definitely weakening.

Paco shook his head impatiently. 'Light!' he repeated, but this time he was pointing back the way they had come. 'I *see* light,' Paco explained, searching for words.

Eric stared at him blankly.

'Give.' He gestured urgently at the torch.

Eric paused. Suppose Paco ran away and left him and Buster alone in the dark. Then he realized that he wouldn't get very far with his trench foot.

Now it was Eric and Buster's turn to follow. Paco took them back the way they had come, flashing the still-weakening torch, successfully remembering the route until they eventually arrived in a large cave. Dull grey light lit the walls and Eric's heart raced.

Above them was a tall chimney in the rock with a small patch of sky at the very top. The first part of the climb looked easy, with ledges as well as nooks and crannies for hands and feet, but further up the chimney the rock was sheer.

'We'll try the tunnels again,' said Eric hopelessly.

He felt completely incapable of tackling such a climb.

Paco, however, was still gazing up the shaft, as if he had not heard him or, more likely, didn't understand. 'We climb,' he said.

'What about Buster?'

'Stay.'

'You'll have to go alone.' Eric was adamant. Buster looked up at him and whined.

Paco took an ammunition belt from around his shoulders and gestured that he wanted to tie Buster to an outcrop of rock.

'No,' said Eric. 'I'll stay with him.' Then he realized he still couldn't trust Paco. Suppose he did get up the chimney, even with his foot, and abandoned them? He and Buster might never be discovered.

'Give me that belt. I'll do it.'

Buster was eventually secured and Eric gazed up at the chimney doubtfully.

'OK?' asked Paco impatiently.

'Yes.' Eric noticed that the young Argentine seemed much calmer now, as if he was living for the moment, wiping out the future.

As they began to climb, Eric could see that Paco was in considerable pain but this didn't slow him up. Uneasily he realized that their positions had been reversed. Paco was in charge now.

They clambered on, breathing heavily, bracing

themselves against the rock wall as it narrowed. Buster barked below, straining at his leash, and then began to howl. Eric tried to comfort himself with the thought that his father knew the Labyrinth in great detail and would soon be able to rescue the old sheepdog, but it was terrible to hear him in such distress.

Eric didn't dare look down at the drop below. If he did that, if he thought too much about Buster's despair, he knew that he would fall. Nevertheless, his whole body began to shake.

Pausing to catch his breath, Eric saw that Paco had reached the sheer side of the chimney. The Argentine hesitated for a second and then, with a series of painful gasps, hauled himself up the rock face, relying on the strength in his wrists.

With a renewed feeling of dread, Eric realized that he was neither tall enough nor strong enough to do the same. He would crash down into the abyss, smashing himself to pieces in front of Buster.

'It's no good,' he shouted up to Paco. 'I can't do it.'

'Come.'

Clinging to the rock Eric gazed up to see that Paco was lying on a ledge, gripping the rock behind him with his legs, the sweat trickling into his eyes, one long arm extended.

'Come,' he said firmly.

'I can't reach,' yelled Eric.

He knew that he had to try. If he climbed slightly

higher, got a strong foothold and pushed himself up, maybe Paco *could* grab him. But wasn't he too heavy? Would he pull Paco off? Then they would both tumble into the abyss.

Eric clambered up a little further and, balancing precariously, stretched up, made fleeting contact with Paco's hand and then clutched at the rock again, somehow steadying himself, sure that he was going to fall.

Buster's howling became louder.

'Don't let me go,' he whispered and then looked up into Paco's pale face. 'Please don't let me go.' Then, with a tremendous effort of will, Eric stood on his toes and stretched up again.

This time they made firmer contact and, although there was a dreadful moment when Eric thought his hand was slipping, Paco's grip on his wrist tightened. He was dragged up, bumping painfully against the rock, the roaring back in his ears.

For a moment Eric had the terrifying sensation of flying as his foot left the crevice. Then he suddenly found his chest scraping the ledge, which was much broader than he had imagined, despite the fact that Paco was taking up a good part of it.

Eric was still in his grip, being pulled along the rock, his legs dangling and then pumping furiously as he tried to get a hold.

He was on his own now, inching himself up, the

exhilaration soaring, blood at his fingertips as he scrabbled at the rock.

At last they lay side by side on the ledge, gasping for breath.

The rest of the climb up towards the hard grey patch of sky was easy, despite the fact that it was made to the accompaniment of Buster's hoarse but still frantic barking.

Finally, Eric followed Paco out on to the tussock grass at the top of the cliff, looking down on the valley of death.

The freezing rain had lessened and mist was blowing in from the sea.

'Let's go home,' said Eric, struggling to his feet. 'My father will fetch Buster.'

But Paco didn't move, and Eric could see that his eyes were glazed with fear.

'You'll be a British prisoner of war.' Eric tried to reassure him. 'Come on. It's my turn to help you.'

He would tell his parents that the Argentine deserter had saved his life and they would pass the information on to the British army. But that was all he could do for him. That was all he could ever do.

Eric began to run down the cliff path with Paco close behind.

RESISTANCE
by Richard Brown

My mother's hand was shaking as she handed me the yellow star.

'What's it for?' I asked, though I could guess. A year ago I would have accepted it from her without question; but since then we'd had to get used to the idea of German troops pouring into Holland, like poison coursing through the veins in our bodies. Now, with Nazi foot-patrols in our streets and the roar of German lorries through the city, I was suspicious of everything.

'We all have to wear them,' she answered, threading a needle.

'Not all,' my father interjected bitterly. 'Just Jews.'

'Why?'

He sighed. 'So we can be recognized.'

That seemed an odd answer to me. I put the star on the table. 'I don't want it,' I said, pushing it away.

My parents glanced at each other. Since Father had had to give up work and had retreated to the flat for almost all of his time, and since Mother had found it increasingly difficult to find food for us, I had been very careful not to add to their troubles. But the star was already hateful to me. 'I'm half-German,' I protested. 'Can't you tell them, Dad, that you're German?'

'Doesn't matter where Jews come from,' said my mother. 'And if they find out I'm English . . .' She shrugged and handed me the needle and thread.

A few minutes later my big sister Lily came in, banging the door behind her. She had recently moved out to be a governess in a rich family's house in the city but she often called in and sometimes stayed the night. Her thick mat of dark curly hair glistened with raindrops. She shook her coat in the hall.

She saw what we were doing and the greeting died on her lips. 'Why?' she asked, tensing.

My father looked ashamed; my mother's face was a mask. 'Here's yours,' she said, holding out another star. Lily's eyes went savage. She snatched the star and threw it on the ground. 'Never,' she said, grinding it with her heel. Turning to me, she said, 'Stop sewing, Anton. That star will kill you.'

Her words created an unholy row. I was torn between my parents' belief that it was safer to conform to whatever the Germans decreed in the hope that they would leave us alone, and Lily's scornful resistance.

My mother got her way as far as I was concerned: the star was sewn on my jacket, directly over my heart. But in the hall Lily whispered to me, 'When you are outside, Anton, hide the star if you can or take off your coat. It makes it easy for them to pick you up and cart you off to one of their death camps. Understand?'

Death camps! Where did Lily get a phrase like that? It made me shiver.

A few weeks later Daniel, my best friend, banged on the door of our apartment. 'They've sealed off our street,' he gasped, his face white, his breath coming in fits and starts. 'I was just coming home but I couldn't get through. What about my mum?'

Daniel lived alone with his mother. His father and two elder brothers had been conscripted into the army and had not been heard of for months.

I raced down the street with Daniel. His house was a few blocks away. Barriers had been erected at either end of his street and German soldiers were going from house to house dragging out Jews and loading them onto lorries. We huddled in a doorway and watched in horror. I'd always run away when this had happened before, thinking: will they come for us one day?

Daniel cried out. We saw his mother being pushed onto a lorry. Daniel was trembling. I had my arms around him from behind to stop him hurtling towards her, to stop him being caught. 'Where are they taking her?' he said. I thought of Lily's death camps.

It was then that I became aware that under my hand was his yellow star. I was shocked. After Lily's warning, I had soon discarded my own.

At the same time I had a curious and creepy feeling that I was being watched. It was as if, suddenly, someone was aware of everything about me, my thoughts, fears, the rapid beat of my heart, the way my hand hid the star. I looked fearfully about me and my gaze locked with that of a German officer a few feet away, sitting in a car. I felt his gaze crawl all over me. Suddenly he opened the car door and climbed out before we had the presence of mind to run.

I could feel Daniel's heart thumping wildly through his coat. I said in my best German, 'Where are they taking them?'

He looked surprised. 'Where did you learn to speak German like that?'

I tried to smile. 'My father's German,' I said. 'He came here years ago to set up a business.' As I had hoped, this bit of information made him think of me not just as a Jew – a body to be deported or starved – but as a German too, one of his own nationality. (I didn't realize until later that for most Gestapo officers this wouldn't have mattered a jot; but I was lucky – this one was different.)

He must have noticed how upset Daniel was. 'He's my cousin,' I said quickly.

He regarded us both with sharp blue eyes. I was about to make a run for it when, glancing back to see that he was not being observed, he whispered, 'Get away from here now.'

We ran all the way home. In the hall of our apartment we doubled up, gasping for breath and still shaken by our narrow escape.

Lily was in the kitchen, unloading a shopping bag. Looking at our faces, she said, 'What's happened?'

Daniel tried to blurt out what we had seen but he was still too out of breath. My parents came in and I told them what had happened. Daniel became very pale; he trembled for hours afterwards, as if in shock.

I shared my bedroom with him that night and he cried into his pillow. As I listened to his sobs I thought of the German officer, the inscrutable look in his sharp eyes, and I wondered why he had whispered that to us, knowing full well that under my hand was Daniel's yellow star.

★

Daniel was fragile and withdrawn during the day, but at night in the dark of our bedroom he talked, telling me everything about his life as if he was trying to preserve it.

One morning he said, 'Do you think it will be safe to go back home?'

'To live there?' I asked, astonished.

He looked at me as if I was stupid. 'Just to get some things.'

We thought the apartment might have been looted, but his mother or a neighbour had had the presence of mind to lock it. Milk had turned sour in a bottle on the table, a half-eaten sandwich was growing mould, flowers were drooping in a vase. Daniel began to sob to himself and I felt awkward. He fetched a bag and hurried around the flat, stuffing into it anything he thought he might need: clothes, books, photographs, a few rations. I stared out of the window into the narrow street. All the windows of the tall houses stared back, blank.

There was a young woman coming up the street. She moved rapidly, almost stealthily, as if she did not want to be noticed. These days that was nothing out of the ordinary, but I knew this woman. I craned over the windowsill to get a better look.

Lily!

What was she doing in this part of the city? I

remembered that it was one of her two half-days off during the week. She had always been mysterious about what she did on those two half-days; she never spent them at home. I didn't call to her — I was curious to find out what she was up to. Further up the street she crossed the road to my side and paused at a door, looked about her, then quickly inserted a key into the lock. She slipped into the house.

I tried to tell Daniel what I had just seen but he wasn't listening. He had decided to leave a note for his family. His voice was so bleak and distant I left him to it and turned back to the window. Tears pricked my own eyes and the breeze made them feel cold.

It took a while for me to understand. 'Boyfriend!' I exclaimed. 'That's it! She's got a boyfriend in there and she doesn't want any of us to know.' Our parents were very strict about that sort of thing.

'Where?' asked Daniel. Having finished his letter, he began to take an interest. I pointed to the house a few doors down.

'When she's gone,' I said, 'let's creep round the back of that house and have a look, yeah?'

Daniel nodded, glad of any diversion.

She left the house soon after, walking rapidly in the opposite direction.

We climbed over a locked gate at the back of the house into an unkempt garden.

I remember thinking I saw a face staring at us from

a neighbour's window – a face that I've wondered about ever since – but I said nothing about it to Daniel.

The downstairs window revealed nothing, no sign of life. I shinned up a rusty fire-escape to the first floor.

There in a bedroom was a young man dozing on the bed. He was very good looking. Trust Lily!

Later that week, when Lily had her second half-day off, I persuaded Daniel to go back with me to his apartment to spy on her again. I had not said anything to Lily about seeing her – I didn't want to spoil her secret. We spent all afternoon watching the street. Few people were about – they felt safer indoors – and the Germans, having 'cleaned up' this street, seemed to have lost interest in it.

Lily did not come.

Frustrated and disappointed, I couldn't bear the thought of just going home. I was thirsting for some excitement. For a dare, I said, 'Let's run past the Gestapo headquarters.' It was the ultimate dare for Jewish boys like me. Daniel's eyes went wide with fear. 'Don't worry,' I said, 'I'll do the talking if anyone stops us.' Daniel no longer wore his yellow star and I had found that my ability to talk good German was a kind of protection.

Out of breath, we reached the tall, bleak, modern

office block that served as the Gestapo HQ. I felt suddenly afraid – of the guards, the building, the street even – and I called off the dare I'd made, much to Daniel's relief. But as I turned to go, I was stopped in my tracks. Coming out of the building, clutching a shopping bag and laughing with one of the guards was – Lily!

My head swam as if the pavement had shifted beneath me. Lily at Gestapo HQ, the most feared and reviled place in the city? I could not understand it.

All the way home we were so deep in speculation about what this could mean that we failed to see a black car parked not far from our apartment.

'Boy,' came a German voice from the car. 'Over here.' The voice ran like an electric shock through me. 'Don't run away. You know me already.' It was the German officer we had spoken to on the day Daniel's mother had disappeared.

I approached the car warily, cautioning Daniel to stay where he was.

I looked into the officer's piercing blue eyes, eyes that gave nothing away.

'Tell Lily,' he said softly, 'Kurt called. To wish her a *very fine evening.*'

I said, 'Is that all?'

'It will be enough,' he said. 'And don't repeat it to anyone else. Understand?'

I nodded.

He gestured towards Daniel. 'Why is your cousin always so silent?' he asked, with a knowing smile. He started up the car and drove off.

I hated the German invaders. But it was harder to hate this one.

Lying on our beds that evening, Daniel and I decided that Lily was either a traitor or a member of the Resistance. I felt in my bones that she wasn't a traitor. So, the Resistance — but what exactly was the Resistance? My father had once explained that there were small groups of people all over the city dedicated to smuggling out Allied airmen who had been shot down behind enemy lines. Some of them infiltrated Gestapo offices and barracks ... It was dangerous work fit only for heroes, hardened fighters: how could Lily, just eighteen and not much bigger than five foot three, be one of them? I just couldn't believe it. But if she wasn't, why did she seem so at home at the Gestapo headquarters?

About eight o'clock I heard Lily come in. I suddenly remembered the German officer in the car.

'Lily,' I whispered standing in the bedroom door-way to catch her as she passed. She looked weary but she gave me a brief smile. 'There was a German officer in the street outside this afternoon.' She stiffened. 'His name is Kurt. He told me to wish you a good evening.'

'A what?' She put her hands on my shoulders, a look of earnest concentration on her face. 'Anton, what were his exact words? Think.'

I recalled them, for they had struck me as slightly odd. '"Tell Lily Kurt called to wish her a very fine evening."'

'My God,' Lily murmured, a look of acute anxiety in her eyes. She stood immobile in the hall for a few seconds, her face tense. 'Don't say anything to anyone about this,' she whispered hoarsely. Then she hurried out; we heard the door slam downstairs.

'Lily's in trouble,' I said to Daniel, who had been listening to all this. 'We've got to help her.'

'How?' said Daniel.

I thought for a moment. 'We can go and tell her boyfriend.'

We hurried through the evening streets. It wasn't safe to be out and, daringly, we had slipped out without my parents' knowledge, knowing they would have stopped us if we'd asked to go out. We kept in the shadows and melted into doorways at the first sound of a passing vehicle. People hurried past, avoiding eye contact.

We thought we might find Lily at her boyfriend's house – in which case we would just slip back home again – but it was silent and dark. Something must have delayed her. This time we knocked on the door. There was no answer. We climbed into the garden again and silently shinned up the fire-escape.

But we were in for a shock! As I climbed through the window, a hand gripped the back of my neck. Another slid over my mouth. I was pulled into the dark bedroom and pushed onto the floor. It was so unexpected, I almost choked with fright. Before Daniel knew what was going on, he was seized too and thrown down beside me.

I struggled into a sitting position and saw in the dim light the young man I'd seen on the bed the other day. He was standing by the window looking nervously out into the garden. I swallowed hard. 'You needn't be afraid of us,' I said. Instinctively, I tried speaking in English first and I could see that he understood me. 'I know who you are,' I added, gaining confidence. He stared at me, surprised. 'You're Lily's boyfriend, aren't you? I'm her brother.'

But he seemed puzzled by my words and, as the moonlight caught the fear in his eyes, something clicked in my mind. I flushed with shame. 'You're . . . You're *not* Lily's boyfriend, are you?' I said, the truth dawning on me. How stupid of me! 'You're on the run. Yes?'

He stiffened. I could almost smell his fear now.

I whispered to Daniel what I had discovered; then

I said, 'We thought Lily would be here. She ran out of the house in such a hurry.'

He made a dismissive gesture with his hand. 'Why do you keep talking of your sister?'

'She's . . .' I was about to say, '. . . in the Resistance, I think,' but I bit back the words just in time – it was something my father said always had to be kept secret. He seemed to understand something of what I was thinking, though, for he muttered 'Felice' to himself, nodding slightly.

'Why was she in such a hurry?' he said with sudden urgency. He lifted me up and dropped me onto the bed.

'Because of the German in the car. Kurt. He said—'

The word 'German' galvanized him. He lifted Daniel up and threw him on the bed beside me, then looked for something to tie us up with. In the wardrobe he found some ties. 'I'm sorry about this,' he said, flexing a tie between his fists. 'I've got to get away from here and I can't risk you giving me away. Your sister will find you soon enough.'

'Where will you go?' I asked, trying to find some way of delaying him in the hope that Lily would turn up and sort everything out.

He shook his head helplessly. I felt his despair.

'He could hide in my flat,' said Daniel, guessing my question. 'They wouldn't look in there again, would they?'

I translated this, explaining why Daniel's flat was now empty.

The Englishman regarded us suspiciously. 'Why should I trust you?' he said, tightening the tie in his hand and stepping towards me.

I thought frantically for a moment. 'We are Jews,' I blurted out. 'Besides, think of Lily . . .'

He considered this for a moment; then his hands dropped to his sides. Daniel and I sat up, watching him hopefully. A car droned by outside and the sound seemed to help him decide. 'OK,' he said, 'show me this flat.'

I whispered to Daniel; he ferreted in his pocket and brought out a key. I said to the Englishman, 'Daniel will take you there, it's only a few houses away. I'll stay here and tell Lily what has happened.'

He didn't want to leave me there, and we argued. H was right, of course – it was foolish to stay there; but I was worried and curious about Lily and I thought I would hang on there for a while in case she came. Just before he followed Daniel out of the window the English soldier touched my arm and said, 'Thank you.' (Even today, as I write this so many years later, I can still feel that touch on my shoulder and it makes me shudder – with guilt, with pity, and with anger too.)

I smoothed the bed and put away the ties and then went downstairs. It was eerie sitting in the dark of the front room – the electricity seemed to be off – with only the moonlight to pick out the shape of the furniture. I thought of Lily, of the secret life she must have been leading, of how she had kept us all in ignorance, and for the first time in my life I even felt a little afraid of her.

After a quarter of an hour of this, flinching at every noise in the street outside, I'd had about as much as I could stand. Perhaps, as the Englishman wasn't her boyfriend, I was wrong to think she would ever have come. What did I really know of her life? I went upstairs, meaning to climb out of the bedroom window and see if Daniel was all right, when I heard footsteps hurrying along the street. They faltered just outside the house, then hurried past, then doubled back, faded, and returned. Was it Daniel? Or a spy? A suspicious neighbour? Or . . . ?

A key turned in the lock. The door opened. There was a pause. Then it closed. Footsteps on the stairs. I simply couldn't move. The bedroom door opened. A torch flashed in my face.

'Anton!'

It was Lily. I nearly collapsed with relief.

'What in God's name are you doing here?' Her voice was shrill with alarm. She flashed the torch about the room.

'He's gone,' I said. 'With Daniel.' I explained what had happened. 'We thought you were in trouble and we couldn't think of anyone to go to for help. Mum and Dad would have been no good.'

She was angry with me, however. 'You should never, *never*, take such risks, Anton. You're only a kid. Now, come on, we've got to get out of here at once. It's dangerous.'

Cautiously, she peered out of the bedroom window; then she drew back with a quick intake of breath. 'I think there's a soldier out there,' she hissed. 'Keep out of sight.' She switched off her torch and we stood on either side of the window. I pressed my hands against the wall to steady myself. 'We'll have to go out by the front door,' she said.

But as we came down the stairs, the street outside was suddenly filled with the sound of engines, tyres screeching, German voices. There was a loud rap on the door. 'Break it down,' someone commanded.

Coolly, Lily opened the door and stood there frowning at two German soldiers, their rifle-butts poised. 'What's all this?' she demanded in German.

An officer stepped out from the shadows and shone his torch into her face so that she had to shield her eyes with her hand. 'Fräulein,' he said, 'don't I know you?'

Lily smiled. 'You should, Major.' She fished for something in her coat and brought out a piece of card. (Afterwards, when I asked her about that, she said that it was a Gestapo HQ card; she had, with amazing courage, infiltrated the nerve centre of the city's Gestapo and had, by passing on information gathered secretly there, saved many Jewish and Allied soldiers' lives. But I didn't know that then and I was confused.)

The major examined the pass. 'Of course,' he said, handing it back. 'But tell me, Felice, what are you doing in this house? It's such a strange coincidence.'

Felice – that name again.

'Coincidence, Major? I don't understand. This house belongs to my aunt. I'm keeping an eye on it while she's away. And I brought my brother along for a bit of company. Is that so strange?'

'Probably some mistake,' he said, shining his torch into my face. 'But now that we are here, I'm sure that you can have no objection if my men take a look around.'

Lily shrugged. 'If you must,' she said. She and I stepped into the street to let the soldiers pass into the house.

I could not help thinking, what if they had turned up half an hour ago? My hands were so clammy with sweat I kept wiping them surreptitiously on my trousers.

We waited patiently, listening to the soldiers ransack the house. Lily kept tapping her foot on the pavement. The major continued to stare at us.

I noticed that apart from the two cars outside the house there was another one parked much further down the street, beyond the door of Daniel's apartment block. It appeared that someone was sitting in it, smoking a cigarette.

Suddenly the noise in the house died down and a voice called the major inside. My heart missed a beat. Had they found some evidence? A moment later the major called Lily in and I heard them go upstairs. I tried to stop myself shaking.

Then a sudden movement in the shadows further down the street caught my eye. A door was opening. A small head was appearing . . . It hesitated, not seeing us, then someone small slipped out. *Daniel!*

There was no time to shout a warning.

Two soldiers saw him and cried, 'Halt!' Daniel froze. Then I found my voice. 'Daniel,' I shouted, and I started to run towards him. The soldiers called to me to halt too. I didn't, but I had the sense to slow down.

Daniel turned and began to run in the opposite direction. As he approached the car at the end of the street, its headlamps suddenly blazed and he was caught in the glare. He stumbled, blinded, and nearly fell. An officer stepped out of the car and seized hold of him.

Daniel could not speak German, he couldn't disguise the fact that he was a Jew or explain what he was doing there. They'd get his address and search his flat and find the Englishman. I stopped in utter despair. *This was my fault.*

Daniel was struggling in the officer's grip. The officer said something to him and he went limp. I felt a sudden spurt of hope. Didn't I know that officer? I took a few more steps towards them.

As I neared them, one of the soldiers behind me got hold of my arm and started to drag me back, cursing. The officer barked an order at him. The soldier let go of me, clipped his heels, saluted and shouted, 'Colonel.'

It was Kurt!

He ordered the soldiers back to the house, then turned on me. 'Do you know where the Englishman is?'

What should I say? Could I trust him? I could see he was angry.

'Tell me,' he urged. 'I cannot save your friend here or your sister unless you tell me.'

Daniel looked at me, terrified. But in my mind I saw the young Englishman too, his taut body trembling slightly in the moonlight, the way his hands had gripped the window sill, the fear in his eye.

This was one of the worst moments of my life – and now, when I think of what must have happened to the Englishman I realize that perhaps it was *the* worst. How could I betray him? But if I didn't . . . I gazed imploringly at Kurt. 'Please don't ask me that,' my gaze said.

Daniel was shaking in the officer's grasp. I thought,

then, of the yellow star on his jacket that I had covered with my hand on the day that they had taken his mother away: it burst, a blaze of light in my mind, like a sign. I turned to look at the door of Daniel's apartment block and slightly inclined my head – two tiny gestures that seemed superhuman to me. I've tried not to hate myself for sacrificing the Englishman, but as Daniel has reminded me again and again, I had no choice.

The officer nodded, let go of Daniel and called the two soldiers back. They burst into Daniel's apartment block. I watched them, feeling sick to the pit of my stomach.

Further up the road Lily and the major appeared on the pavement. Whatever they had found in the house, Lily must have been able to explain it away.

Kurt turned back to us. 'Run,' he said. 'Get away now. We've got what we came for. I'll do my best for your sister.'

I didn't like leaving Lily but Daniel was already pulling me away. And I wanted to thank Kurt, but there was no time. Twice he had saved our lives; he was what my father called 'a good German'. 'There are many of us,' I remember him saying, 'but we have to do our good deeds in secret now.'

We turned the corner at the end of the street. I stopped, panting hard. I had to see what was going to happen. It was difficult trying to make out anything in the darkness, but as Lily and the major approached Kurt standing in the light of the car's headlamps, there was a commotion in the apartment block doorway. The soldiers dragged out the Englishman, who was struggling and shouting.

My heart was in my mouth. I realized at once – as Lily must have done – that if he called my sister's name or gave any sign that he knew her, she would be arrested too. And I would never see her again . . . They would come for my parents, for me, for Daniel . . . Such calamities, flashing through my brain, made me feel suddenly so sick with fear that I bent over and retched, though I brought up nothing but a greenish liquid.

When I looked again, Kurt was standing between Lily and the prisoner; he was shielding her. The Englishman was dragged up the road and put into one of the cars. 'I'm sorry,' I whispered again and again to myself.

I watched Lily get into Kurt's car. Then Daniel and I ran back home.

Life in the city was too dangerous for us now, so Lily used her contacts in the Resistance to get us smuggled out. My parents, Daniel and I left with her two nights later, carrying small bundles of our most precious things, and we were smuggled from one house to another. We spent days in dark, smelly trucks or hiding in remote farms. The journey through Belgium and France was a nightmare – I've blocked much of it from my mind – and it was only the Resistance that got us through. The Red Cross helped us to cross the Swiss border.

During the journey I tried to apologize to Lily for the danger we had put her in, but she brushed my efforts aside. 'Remember, Anton,' she said, 'if you and Daniel hadn't got the English soldier out of the house, I might have been caught with him there by the Germans. That alone saved me.'

That made me feel a little better. 'But I wish I could have saved the soldier too.'

'Of course you do,' she said, stroking my cheek soothingly. 'But you were asked to choose between him and Daniel. That was a terrible thing to have to face, but you made the right choice.'

A little later, turning the events over in my mind, I asked her, 'Why did it take you so long to get to the house that night?'

Lily sighed. 'I was arranging an escape route for the Englishman. It was all set up but I had to activate it. Now, no more questions. You have a new life ahead of you, you and Daniel; think of that instead.'

LEAVING SARAJEVO
by Judith Hemington

Ahmed looked out of the window of the plane, and rows of ugly little houses in straight lines tilted first one way, then another, and queues of toy-sized cars seemed hardly to move at all.

The air hostess caught his eye. 'We'll be landing very soon. I'll see you out to the family you're staying with.' She spoke slowly, so Ahmed could understand what she said.

He nodded. He wanted to thank her, but he felt too miserable for that. If only he could just hide on the plane and then fly back to where he'd come from. He didn't want to be in England. He longed to be with his mother in Sarajevo, and for his elder brother and his father to be there too, and for everything to be as

49

it was before the terrible war started.

For months and months when he had gone out in the streets he had run fast, his stomach tight with fear. But even so, he wanted to be back. He wanted to be waiting with his mother for his brother and his father to come home from the fighting that had swept them away.

When the letter arrived Mamma had cried and said how kind the people were to offer. She'd miss him so much, she said, but he must go.

'I don't want to go!' he had shouted.

'I want one of my sons to be safe,' Mamma said, and so he was here, almost in London, dreading meeting a family he didn't know. He still didn't quite understand why they had written. His mother said it was something to do with his grandfather – he wasn't sure what.

When the fighting began the English family had posted some food parcels, but only two had got through. The rest had been stolen. It was a shame about that, because there was hardly any food around in Sarajevo.

A few months had passed while papers were sorted out, and now here he was.

The plane shuddered and roared, and Ahmed felt sick with unhappiness.

There was a bewildering sea of faces behind the barrier. Ahmed blinked, and then caught sight of a cluster of people holding up his name in big letters. Without speaking he pointed the air hostess in the direction of the family, and she looked relieved, and hurried over.

Mr Feldman shook his hand. Mrs Feldman hugged him, but Ahmed held stiffly back. She wasn't his mother. There was a boy called Simon, who kept his eyes on his feet and said 'Hello' very quickly. He was about the same age as Ahmed, eleven or twelve, he thought. His sister was younger and was called Becky. She smiled in a friendly way and talked so fast Ahmed couldn't understand what she was saying.

They had a large, silver car – a Volvo – and Ahmed sank down in the back with Simon and Becky. Simon asked him what football club he supported, and Becky said: 'Oh no, don't talk about football, it's so boring!'

Ahmed didn't want to talk about anything. Sadly he stared out of the window. England seemed so different from Sarajevo.

'You're sharing a room with Simon,' Mrs Feldman said. 'I hope you don't mind.'

Ahmed had the feeling that Simon didn't particularly want to share with him. That made it worse.

'What would you like to do after supper?' Becky asked.

'Don't badger him. One thing at a time,' Mrs

Feldman said. Ahmed didn't know what 'badger' meant.

'I expect you'd like to phone your mother to say you've got here safely.'

Ahmed's large brown eyes were full of gratitude as he turned to Mrs Feldman. 'Yes, yes – I would like that,' he said.

But the phone was in the kitchen, and the family were around. Mamma's voice sounded strange. He told her he wanted to come home, and she said he mustn't say that. He could feel tears coming into his eyes, so he couldn't carry on talking. He couldn't bear it if the family saw him crying. Mamma said she wanted to thank Mrs Feldman, so he handed the receiver to her, then rushed up to his room. He'd wasted the chance to talk, and now it was all over, and perhaps there wouldn't be another time.

For a while he sat on the bunk bed, breathing slowly, trying to force the unhappiness back down. After a time Simon's face appeared around the door. 'Supper's ready!' he said, and left before Ahmed had time to reply.

Ahmed tried to eat, but the food didn't taste like food at home. Each mouthful got stuck in his throat and refused to go down without several attempts at swallowing.

The family conversation around the table seemed to be happening far away. He could understand some things, but not all. His father was a musician and had travelled abroad with his orchestra. He could speak some English, and he had taught Ahmed. They could get some English programmes on the radio, too, and his family had listened to these. 'You must learn English!' his father was always saying. Ahmed picked things up quickly, but he found it much more difficult to understand what people were saying now he was in England. People talked so fast. It was too much effort to take it all in, so his mind wandered off. He kept picturing the day his father had to go away to fight, and his brother, and how empty the apartment seemed once they'd gone. There were some pictures that crept into his mind that were so terrible that he tried to push them away. There was the day a shell had landed near the bread shop. He had been standing so close to that spot only the day before. Everyone knew someone who had been killed and everyone was shocked and scared, and nobody went out unless they had to.

In Sarajevo he'd felt so hungry all the time, and now, there was food on the table and he had no appetite to eat.

After supper Mrs Feldman suggested Ahmed might like to go up with Simon to his room. Simon had pulled a face and, without speaking, had started walking towards the stairs. Ahmed wasn't sure whether he was expected to follow him, but he did.

53

'What d'you want to do?' Simon asked in a resentful voice.

Ahmed shrugged. What could he say?

'I'm watching TV,' Simon said, switching on the set in his room and fixing his eyes on the screen.

Ahmed wished Simon could be more friendly, but he was quite glad to have the television on. Although he couldn't really understand what was happening, except that the film was about policemen and crooks, at least with the television on he could just let everything flow over him. It wouldn't matter that he didn't understand.

That night when Simon switched the light off Ahmed lay stiffly in his bed and couldn't sleep. Simon was in the top bunk above him: Ahmed could hear him breathing, and he didn't want to toss and turn in case he was a nuisance.

The next day he stayed at home while Simon and Becky went to school. In the evening Simon's friend came, and he and Simon played games together, leaving Ahmed out. He didn't really want to be included, because he couldn't follow what they said to each other, but he wished they wouldn't make him feel so unwelcome. Becky was more friendly, but Ahmed didn't really want to be with her either.

'Simon will take you around at school, when you're not in lessons,' Mrs Feldman said on the day they decided he should go for the first time.

But it didn't work out quite like that. When they arrived at the school Ahmed was in a daze. He understood some of the things people said to him, but all the complicated instructions about where he should be, and when – all that was so difficult to follow. He was to attend classes with some other children who didn't speak English well, and a teacher told a boy called Michael to look after him.

'See you at break!' Simon said, but after he'd run off Ahmed realized that Simon hadn't told him where to meet. At the end of the two lessons Ahmed hoped the teacher would tell him where Simon would be, but he didn't, and Ahmed didn't like to ask.

'I see Simon now?' Ahmed said to Michael, who assumed that Ahmed knew what to do, and went off to be with his friends.

There were so many children streaming down staircases, hurrying along corridors, laughing and shouting. Ahmed felt panic rising inside him. Once he'd had a nightmare that he'd lost the rest of his family at the market in Sarajevo, and he felt as he felt then. Hopelessly he stepped out into the yard, threading his way through dense crowds. There was no chance of finding Simon in the crush of people. After a time he saw a teacher walking towards him, and he decided to ask her if she knew where Simon was.

'Sorry!' she said. 'Can't help. Try at the office,'

and she pointed vaguely behind her, then rushed on.

Ahmed noticed a tall boy with very short fair hair and bulging eyes staring at him in an unfriendly way, so he moved quickly on, hoping he'd find the office without trouble. Behind him he heard footsteps. His neck tensed, and he walked faster. He didn't turn back to look. Then the footsteps behind him quickened their pace, and soon he found himself being nudged against the wall.

'Where you from?' the boy asked, putting his arm in front of Ahmed to prevent him from moving forward.

'I am from Sarajevo,' Ahmed said in a quick, quiet voice.

'What's that?' the boy asked.

Ahmed repeated what he'd said. He backed away from the boy, and a radiator pressed against his spine.

'We don't like foreigners here,' the boy said, his voice full of spite.

Ahmed was holding his breath, hoping for something to happen, something to allow him to escape.

A teacher came hurrying around a corner and, seeing him, the boy moved swiftly away. For a moment Ahmed remained where he was, trembling a little from the shock of what had happened. Then wandered towards the office. Now he hated the school even more.

His eye strayed towards a glass door, and beyond that to tall gates, and a road. A loud buzzer sounded, and there was a stirring and scrambling to classes. Ahmed didn't know where he was meant to be next. It all seemed too complicated. Quietly he slipped out of the glass door, across the yard, and out of the gates. On the street the atmosphere seemed gentler and much less frantic than in the school. A little way down the road there was a bus stop. He joined a queue of people there, and before long a bus appeared.

A strange feeling had come over him. It was as if he were in a trance. He knew that he shouldn't be doing this – just travelling into the unknown, but he wanted to get away from that building with the unfriendly people and the conversations he didn't understand.

He gave the driver a coin. The man asked him a question. Ahmed nodded, and the man gave him a ticket. He wasn't sure where he would get off. Perhaps when most other people got off he would leave with them.

After a mile or so there were shops on either side, and the traffic was thicker. A number of people were edging out of their seats, so Ahmed rose and moved towards the door too. When the bus stopped, he got off, and then stood for a minute, bewildered, on the pavement. There were so many things in the shop windows. So different from Sarajevo.

His hand closed around the money in his pocket that Mrs Feldman had given him for his lunch. Already he was feeling hungry, but he decided he should wait before he bought anything to eat. As he walked along he avoided catching people's eyes. He thought they were looking at him strangely, but he didn't want to glance at them to check if this was just his imagination.

After he'd strolled around the shops for some time he caught sight of a McDonald's. He couldn't resist. He had to go in. Perhaps he wouldn't have enough money.

The girl who served him was friendly and helped him to sort out the coins for a Big Mac and French fries. They tasted delicious. Inside McDonald's he felt safe and comfortable, and so he stayed there for as long as he could.

When he came out it had started to drizzle, so he went into a large department store, and when that became boring, he slipped into another. Anxiety began to creep into his mind and spread throughout his body. What was he going to do? How was he to get back to the Feldmans' house? He didn't know where he was. It had been a stupid idea to leave the school. Where had he picked up the bus? Dusk was falling, and as the lights went on the place seemed different from when he'd arrived.

His mind was a blank. He stood still on the pave-

ment, trying to force himself to think clearly. In front of him was a newspaper shop, and as he glanced at the stand outside the shop he saw a familiar name staring at him. Sarajevo. He looked more closely. There was a picture of bodies scattered over the ground. What had happened?

Panic began to take over. He needed to ring his mother . . . make sure she was all right. Wildly he looked around for a phone. He had to reach her. Soon. He couldn't bear not to know.

On the other side of the road he saw a kiosk, so he raced across and wrenched open the door. And then he realised that he probably hadn't enough money, and he didn't know how the phones worked.

Frantically his hand searched his pocket, and out came a little change. It was worth a try. Carefully he read the instructions, then lifted the receiver and dialled. The first time around he heard nothing. He tried again, and there was a ringing tone. All he needed was to hear his mother's voice. Just one word, to know she was safe.

No-one answered. He waited and waited, then stumbled out of the phone box. Now what? He felt very much alone. On the corner of the street he saw a policeman chatting to a motorist. He remembered his mother telling him that British policemen were friendly. Could he ask him to help him to find the Feldmans' house? How would *he* know?

He decided against it but then, after he'd walked past, he changed his mind and came back. A pressing sense of urgency was building up inside him. He needed to get back to the Feldmans' to try to phone his house in Sarajevo.

The policeman listened carefully to what Ahmed said. 'Let me see if I can help you,' he said, and he spoke quickly into his radio. 'I see. Right.' Then he waited. After a while he spoke again. He glanced at Ahmed. 'I think it's the one. Yes. Yes. That's a bit of luck. If you send someone round . . . Corner of Beacon Street – near McDonald's. Right.

'Well, my lad, you've certainly got a lot of people very worried about you! If you come with me we'll take you back where you need to be.'

Ahmed bit his lip, anxious about having caused a lot of trouble, but relieved that he wasn't going to be lost in this unknown part of London for ever.

After a short while he saw a police car winding its way through the traffic. 'There it is!' the policeman said triumphantly. 'In you go, son. The driver can't hold the traffic up for long.'

As he sat in the back of the car his stomach turned over. Mr and Mrs Feldman would dislike him for this. They'd wish they hadn't arranged for him to come. Perhaps they'd send him back. Simon would be even more unfriendly. Then he remembered the picture in the newspaper of all those people lying on the ground in Sarajevo and he was sick with fear.

The car journey seemed to take a long time, but when the car stopped in front of the Feldmans' house Ahmed didn't want to get out.

A light appeared in the hall, the front door opened, and Mr and Mrs Feldman rushed down the drive. Ahmed hung back by the police car, his eyes on the ground. And then a wonderful thing happened. Mr and Mrs Feldman didn't yell at him or even speak to him in a stern voice. They both just hugged him tightly, as if he really mattered. Then Mrs Feldman said softly, 'Oh, Ahmed, you're safe! What a relief! We were so worried.'

'I'm sorry,' Ahmed whispered. 'So sorry I cause trouble.'

'Never mind. The important thing is you're back,' they said.

The Feldmans and Ahmed thanked the policemen, who drove off, and Ahmed followed Mr and Mrs Feldman into the house. Becky came rushing out of the kitchen, Simon behind her. 'Ahmed, I thought you'd got mugged or run over by a bus!' she said. 'What happened? Everyone was going crazy with worry.'

'All in good time,' Mrs Feldman said. 'I expect Ahmed just wants to settle down in the warm with some food.'

Ahmed gave her a grateful smile. All he could think of now, though, was of that newspaper picture. 'Please – I'm sorry I trouble you with one more, but could I phone Sarajevo, please? I saw in the newspaper a picture . . .' He stopped, not sure how to explain.

'Oh yes, of course you'd be worried,' Mr Feldman said. 'It was on the news. You try phoning now.'

Ahmed felt his heart thumping inside him while he dialled. If there was no reply again, he didn't know what he was going to do. His fingers trembled as he picked out all the numbers.

He held his breath, and waited, and waited. Then suddenly there was his mother's voice at the other end. And joy came swilling into his head like an enormous wave.

He didn't stay on the phone long. He didn't need to, now he knew she was OK.

As he walked from the kitchen to the sitting room Simon came up behind him and tapped him on the shoulder. Ahmed turned round, surprised.

'I'm sorry I've been a bit mean since you came,' Simon whispered. 'I was fed up because Mum and Dad didn't ask me whether I minded sharing my room. It wasn't your fault, I know, but . . . I felt really bad when you ran off from school. I thought it was probably because of me – and if anything had happened to you it would have been my fault. When you turned up I was so glad! Shall we be friends now?'

Ahmed didn't understand every word that Simon had said, but he knew that he was being much more friendly now. He smiled at him, and shook the hand that Simon offered to him.

Then in the sitting room he drank a cup of cocoa and tried to explain to the Feldmans what had happened.

'Typical Simon not telling Ahmed where to meet him!' Becky said scornfully.

'No – not Simon. Perhaps I just not understand,' Ahmed said quickly, not wanting to get Simon into trouble.

'That's right – it isn't anybody's fault. It's that terrible war causing all the problems,' Mr Feldman said.

Later that evening, just before Ahmed was going to bed, Mr Feldman put his arm round his shoulder and steered him towards the sofa. 'Come and sit down here next to me – I want to tell you something,' he said.

Ahmed looked at him, wondering what he was going to say.

'My father came from Yugoslavia, as it was then – Zagreb,' Mr Feldman began.

'My grandfather came from Zagreb too,' Ahmed said, 'and then he comes to Sarajevo.'

'I know,' Mr Feldman said. 'And if it hadn't been for

your grandfather, I wouldn't be here today. I expect you know about the Second World War.' Ahmed nodded. 'Well, my father's family were Jewish, and they were in a lot of danger when the Germans invaded that part, and your grandfather, who was a very brave man, hid my father's family, and he helped him escape from the country. Your grandfather and mine were both musicians, just as your father is. They played in the same orchestra. He risked his life for my father. My family have never forgotten that. So, as you can imagine, you're very welcome here, Ahmed. We owe a lot to your family!'

That night when Ahmed went to bed he thought about what Mr Feldman had said, and he was proud of his grandfather and much more at ease in the Feldmans' house. There was another thing to be happy about too. His mother's voice, telling him she was far away from the shell when it exploded. He'd feel homesick again, for sure, but at least he felt much better tonight than he had since he'd arrived. He knew he was welcome.

SARDINES
by Adèle Geras

When you hear the word 'war', what do you think of? Bombs exploding, guns blazing, buildings on fire, soldiers in metal helmets running and running in the shadow of high walls? Or men wearing green uniforms creeping through dense jungle, clutching fearsome silver weapons to their sides? Perhaps your war is airborne: thin, whining planes wheeling through the sky, paratroopers floating to the ground. Maybe the word makes you think of children left orphaned, and lines of refugees tramping through the snow, their houses in ruins, their lives shattered. That's the way war looks in the movies, and if your taste is for more old-fashioned sorts of battles, then you can imagine sword-fights, and cannons and soldiers dressed up in splendid gold-braided jackets riding horses that gallop across the screen and almost into your lap.

My war wasn't like that at all. When I say 'my war' I don't mean I fought in it. I was very young, but there is more than one way of being brave, and more than one way to be a coward. I remember as if it was yesterday not the shooting, and not even the hunger, but what happened when Uncle Michah arrived with two tins of sardines.

There's something else about wars. You have to explain who is fighting, and what it's all about and where it is, so that everyone knows whose side they're on. This war happened in 1948, in a country which was then called Palestine. It was fought, as many other wars have been fought, between Jews and Arabs. My family is Jewish, and we lived in Jerusalem, which was besieged. This meant that Arab troops had formed a ring around the city and no food could reach the shops. We were hungry. I don't mean peckish, or fancying a bite to eat, but truly, painfully hungry. If we had a loaf of bread in the house, it had to last a week. Sugar lumps were like gold, and grocers learned to slice cheese so thinly that you could almost see through it.

We lived in a big, square block of flats. My mother and my father and I were on the third floor. I have no brothers or sisters. This meant that my parents were forever fussing about me, worrying over me, and spoiling me, too, though of course I didn't think of it like that. I was molly-coddled. I realize now, looking back, that my mother hardly ate at all, and that most of the food that came into our flat ended up in my stomach. Still, I spent a lot of time thinking about meals, and looking forward to the delicious things we were going to eat when the fighting was over.

Apart from the hunger, the war everyone was so concerned about hardly touched me at all, except at night. I wasn't allowed to wander the streets unless I was with my parents, it's true, but I had everything I needed, everything that made me happy right there in my block of flats, and I can even give it a name: the Greenbergs.

Their flat was on the floor below ours, and I envied them because they were such a big family. Three brothers, two sisters (one of whom was my special friend Naomi), a mother and a father and a grand-mother. I thought the grandmother was scrawny and sharp-tongued, and I didn't like her very much, even though she made the best stuffed cabbage in Jerusalem. There were also all sorts of cousins and uncles and aunties who wandered in and out of the flat at all hours of the day and night.

We played wonderful games, all through those days. We weren't allowed up on to the flat roof of the building, because there was a chance of a sniper's bullet ricocheting off a wall somewhere and hitting us. The Arab troops were very close. If we *had* been allowed up there, we could easily have seen them. So we had to play in the flat and on the balcony at the back. Danny, the second brother, was brave and cheeky, and always getting into trouble for one thing or another. Naomi and I admired him, and followed his lead in everything. He was also the best at inventing games. We picked leaves from the trees outside and mashed them up with water and made magic potions; we used the black and yellow squares on the floor to play a kind of hopscotch; we made tents out of blankets and played doctors and nurses with Mrs Greenberg's scarves for bandages. We had fun. The war was something that went on somewhere in the grown-up world, although of course we talked about it a lot, mainly at night.

Everything is scarier at night – have you noticed that? Things that never bother you in daylight turn into nightmares. For instance: during the day, jeeps and lorries drove around the streets, and I never even looked at them, but at night they became huge metal monsters with fierce, glowing eyes, and they growled and roared up the streets outside and I trembled and quaked, and wondered if one of them might crash right through the wall of the shelter where we used to spend many of the night-time hours. All the worst shooting went on at night, so everyone who lived in

the flats had to go down and sit for hours in the
shelter, which was just another name for the front
entrance of the flats. This could have been very boring
and also very frightening, but I always sat with Naomi
and Danny, and the rest of the Greenberg children,
and we managed to giggle and chatter so much that
sometimes the other, older residents of the flats had to
tell us to be quiet. It was in the shelter that I first heard
about Uncle Michah.

Naomi said: 'Dafna, my Uncle Michah is coming
tomorrow. Have you ever seen him?'

'I don't know,' I said. 'What does he look like?' The
Greenbergs had so many relatives that I found it hard
to remember all their names, and work out which one
was which.

'He's hairy,' said Danny.

'And fat,' said Naomi.

'He's a hero,' Danny added. 'He's one of the fighters.
He even wears a uniform.'

'But sometimes when he comes he brings food,'
Naomi said. 'Do you remember, last time he brought
oranges? Two oranges. They were so juicy. I wish I had
an orange now. I could eat a whole orange all by
myself.'

I *did* remember the oranges. My mother said at the
time: 'How kind of Mrs Greenberg to let you have a
piece of orange. She has so many children of her own,
and yet she finds a segment for you. A wonderful

woman. Here, take this and go downstairs and tell her I say thank you.' My mother put a quarter of an onion wrapped in newspaper into my hand.

It didn't seem like a very thrilling gift to me, but Mrs Greenberg was delighted. 'How wonderful! We can have soup . . . a quarter of an onion and some salt – you would be amazed how good it can taste. Such a shame we have no bread to dip into it!'

'Maybe,' Naomi said, 'he'll bring sweets. We had an aniseed ball each once. It changed colour. It took ages to suck.'

'Mine lasted almost all night,' said Danny. 'I wish I had one now.'

'Listen,' said Mr Birnbaum, who lived in one of the first-floor flats. 'They're shelling the bank. I'm sure they are. Listen, can you hear them?'

We listened, and the booming of the mortars shook the building. The yellow lights of the lorry-monsters shone briefly on the walls of the shelter as they drove past. A baby started to cry.

'Go to sleep,' my mother said. 'Try and shut your ears to the guns.'

I *did* try, but it was hard. We were lying on blankets and cushions on the stone floor, and apart from the guns and the baby and the whispers of other people, there was the hunger. It's very difficult to go to sleep with nothing in your stomach at all. I closed my eyes and thought about Uncle Michah and what he might bring.

Next day Naomi ran upstairs to find me. 'Quick!' she cried. 'He's here. Come and see what he's brought.'

'Tell me,' I said.

'No,' said Naomi. 'It's a surprise . . . oh, it's wonderful! Come quickly.'

We clattered down to the Greenbergs' flat. The door was open, and even before we were inside I could hear someone's voice (it *had* to be Uncle Michah – no-one else in the Greenberg family sounded like that) growling like a bear.

'I'm frightened,' I whispered to Naomi.

'Nonsense,' she said. 'It's only Uncle Michah. He's nothing to be scared of.'

I followed her into the dining room. Uncle Michah was sitting at the table, drinking tea from a glass that looked tiny and fragile in his gigantic paw. I knew he was a person and not a bear really, but that was what he looked like to me. Danny had said he was fat, and Naomi had told me he was hairy, but nothing they'd said had prepared me properly. He was the biggest man I have ever seen, even sitting down. His shoulders blocked the light from the window. His feet, in black boots, seemed to cover the floor. He overflowed the chair he sat in. He was clean shaven, but you could see the thick black hair on his chest in the opening of his shirt. His hands too, which I couldn't stop thinking of as paws, were covered in hair. I stood rooted to the spot, too terrified to speak.

'Who's this?' he said to Naomi, and to me: 'Tell me your name, little friend of my niece.'

'Dafna,' I said, and I said it so quietly that he asked me again, and I had to repeat myself. I stared at the floor all through this exchange. I felt that if I had to look into those bear's eyes, I would faint.

'Well, girls,' he said, 'look at what I've brought for supper.'

I glanced at the table, and there they were. Two tins of sardines lay on the oilcloth. My mouth filled with saliva at the sight of the silver fish pictured on the label. I thought of the salty taste of them, the smooth, delicious olive oil they floated in coating the inside of my mouth. I swallowed.

'Lovely!' I said to Naomi, and Uncle Michah said:

'Come, girls, into the kitchen. You have to help me divide these sardines up fairly, so that everyone has the same amount. It's not as easy as you think. The fish are wide at the top, and narrow at the bottom, so we have to be very clever, and make all sorts of adjustments. I will need your help.'

In the kitchen, Mrs Greenberg had laid out twelve plates.

Uncle Michah opened the tins, using the little tin-opener key stuck to the side of each tin. He did this carefully, slowly, daintily. 'This oil is too precious,' he said. 'I mustn't spill any of it. We'll lay all the sardines out here on this big plate, and then you can begin to cut them up, girls. We can discuss exactly how many pieces when we've counted the fishes.'

There were ten sardines. There were twelve plates. Each person could have just less than one sardine. We talked about how to divide them.

'Give the children one each,' said Mrs Greenberg, 'and we'll divide the other four fish between the adults.' I noticed that she included me among the children.

'No,' said Uncle Michah. 'Everyone must have the same. We will do it all fairly.'

It took a long time but, in the end, everyone agreed that the sardines had been cut up in the best possible way. We carried the plates into the dining room, and set them round the table. Naomi's brothers and sisters were also there, helping their mother to prepare for the evening meal. One brought glasses from the cupboard, another took the knives and forks out of the drawer, someone else arranged the napkins next to each plate. We were all laughing and happy. People were wandering in and out of the dining room. This meal was going to be something of a feast, thanks to Uncle Michah's sardines.

When I look back at what happened next, I cannot find any explanation for my behaviour. I was hungry, but then so was everyone else. I'm not a daring person, even now, and in those days I was timid and shy. I was the sort of child who was too scared of almost everything to be naughty. The dining room was empty. Suddenly, everyone was somewhere else and I was quite alone. The table stretched out before me like a white desert, and the twelve plates seemed to shine and dazzle me. The fragrance of the sardines drifted up to my nose, and the whole room shimmered. I could hear voices, but they sounded to me at that moment as if they were miles away. My hand moved by itself, as though it had nothing to do with me at all. It snaked out from my side, and picked up the two small pieces of fish on the plate in front of me. Before I could blink, I had crammed them into my mouth and swallowed them. I ran from the room, with the taste of sardines rich on my tongue and my fingers covered in oil. I hid in the lavatory until I thought it was safe to come out, and then I went to the bathroom. I used lots and lots of soap. I made mountains of fluffy white lather, but it seemed to me as I dried my hands that the smell of sardines still clung to my flesh. By the time I got back to the dining room, they were all there, the crime had been discovered, and the hunt was on for the culprit. Everyone was talking at once:

'It couldn't have been an adult.'

'Why not? Since when are adults good at resisting temptation?'

'Danny, was it you?'

'No, no, it wasn't – I promise it wasn't.'

'Didn't anyone see anything?'

'Where were you?'

The scrawny granny spoke into a silence: 'You can all say what you like – Danny is the only one in the family who would be quick enough and naughty enough to do such a thing. Danny, I'm ashamed of you.'

'But . . .' Danny was bright red in the face. He couldn't find words to answer such an accusation.

Then Uncle Michah said: 'Stop! Isn't the war going on outside our windows enough for you? Do we have to have a battle in our own dining room? We are not talking about diamonds here, we are talking about pieces of sardine. Everyone sit down at once. Sit down in front of a plate. I shall have the empty plate. I am the fattest. I can live very well without sardines.'

We sat. We ate. Slowly. I don't know how the fish tasted to everyone else. Maybe they loved every tiny mouthful. I felt as though my mouth was full of clay. I could hardly bring myself to swallow my portion. I couldn't look at anything except my plate. When the sardines had gone, I stared at the flower painted on the china until the image began to blur. I thought the meal would never end, but at last we were allowed to leave the table. I made an excuse, saying I had to go back to my own flat, and ran upstairs as though all the devils in hell were after me.

That night, in the shelter, I could see that Danny

was still in disgrace with some of the Greenberg family. He didn't speak to me at all. He crouched in a corner, and turned his face away. Uncle Michah was there as well. He sat with his back against the wall, and looked to me just like a hulking monster in his cave. The guns began. The lorries went up and down outside. Gradually, everyone fell asleep, but I was wide awake. What I had done grew and swelled in the darkness, and I felt worse and worse: a thief, and not only a thief, but a terrible coward. And not only a coward, but someone who gets one of her very best friends into trouble and says nothing. All around me, people were risking their lives, being shot at, wounded, even killed, and I didn't dare confess to stealing two pieces of sardine. I looked at Naomi. She was fast asleep. My mother and father were snoring slightly. I stood up. No-one moved. I picked my way over the stretched-out bodies to where Uncle Michah was sitting. I thought that because he was sitting up, he must be awake, but he was not. I had to reach out and poke him in the shoulder.

His eyes flew open at once. 'Who is it? What's the matter?' he said. 'Oh, it's you . . . Dafna, isn't it? Naomi's little friend.'

'Yes,' I said. 'I'm sorry to wake you up.'

'That's quite all right – is there anything the matter?'

'Yes,' I whispered. 'I can't sleep.'

'Why not?' he said. 'Is your mother here, in the

shelter? Shouldn't you tell her? I don't know what I can do to help you.'

'I want,' I said, 'to tell you something.'

'Tell me, then.'

'It wasn't Danny who took the sardines today.'

'Really?' Uncle Michah looked at me, and his eyes glittered in the half-light of the shelter.

'Yes,' I said. 'I know who took them. I want to tell you.'

'I won't tell anyone,' said Uncle Michah. 'You may be sure of that. As far as I'm concerned the whole thing is in the past.'

'I took them,' I said, and burst into tears.

Uncle Michah put a hairy bear arm around me, and instead of shrinking away from him in horror, I sobbed onto his shoulder. 'Don't cry,' he said. 'It's nothing, really. I think it's very brave and honest of you to confess. I promise I won't tell a soul. But I also promise that everyone will know Danny had nothing to do with it – that's what's worrying you, isn't it? I can see that it is. Dry your eyes now and go back to your place and try to sleep. I'll bring something else that's nice to eat next time I come, and you shall have your share.'

I didn't feel brave, but I felt very happy. I slept at once, and dreamed of Uncle Michah carrying baskets of food into the shelter.

The siege ended, and the victory parade passed right by our flats. We were all on the balcony to cheer,

and sing songs, and look at the gallant soldiers marching along, happy to be alive still, smiling. Food had
reached the city at last, and we threw oranges down
for the marching men, to say thank you for fighting
for us; thank you for letting us be here today, in the
sunshine, and not at war any more.

I learned many things in the shelter that night.
Most importantly, I learned to judge people by their
actions, and not by what they look like. I also learned
that you can put things right after you have done
something wrong. I learned not to take things like
plentiful food for granted, but I still cannot eat
sardines. Even to think of them makes me feel sick.

WAR GAMES
by Paul Lewis

Tommy gripped the rifle in both hands and strained to listen as he crept through the Bosnian forest. He was the last of his unit to attempt the journey out of the trees to safety. Three had made it. One had been shot and killed by hidden snipers.

It was May, the sun like a molten ball of lava. Tommy could feel the sweat run down his back as he paused for breath, pressing against the trunk of a huge oak tree for cover. He could hear birdsong, the drone of insects, the whisper of a breeze through the branches high above, the distant boom of heavy artillery.

If anyone waited nearby he had no way of knowing, but it would be dangerous to assume he was alone.

One false step and it would be over for him.

It had taken Tommy nearly ten minutes to make it this far into the woods. Squinting ahead, directly into the sun, he could see where the trees ended and the old farm building lay in stone-scattered ruin. That was his target. If he could make it there without being hit then he was out of harm's way and in with a chance of victory.

He used his handkerchief to wipe sweat from his eyes. A few seconds more and he would have to press on. It was tempting to stay where he was, to let the Serbs come to him, but Tommy knew he had to try.

'Come on, thickhead! We've been waiting half the day for you!'

The echoing cry snapped Tommy out of his day-dream. He looked down. The rifle in his hand was just a length of fallen branch. Suddenly he was not hearing heavy artillery but the soft crump of explosions in the quarry two miles away. The Serbs in the woods were only Robbie Fisher and his gang, waiting to pelt him with pine cones as he hurtled towards the old farm. It was their game. Their war game.

Four of Fisher's team had made it through the woods unscathed. Tommy's had scored three out of four. As leader he was last to go. He was only a few hundred metres away from squaring the game. All he had to do was clear his mind and sprint as fast as he could, ducking and weaving to confuse the enemy aim.

Except clearing his mind was impossible.

'Move it!' another voice called.

All right, Tommy thought. He could wait no longer. It was time to go, even though he did not feel like taking part any more. He had no idea where the enemy were hiding. It was no use trying to guess their strategy. Tommy took a deep breath and began to run.

Something small shot straight across the front of his face, so fast it was little more than a blur, hitting a tree to his left with a dull *thwack*. Another pine cone sailed over his shoulder but he did not dare slow to try to pinpoint where it had come from. His heart was hammering in his chest. Heat made it difficult to breathe. All he could hear was a rapid thudding as he raced along the forest path.

He felt something hit even as Fisher's voice boomed out. 'One!'

That was OK. First strike was a flesh wound. You could keep going. Tommy sucked in deep gulps of air and forced himself to run faster. The old farm seemed to grow in size with every step he took. Not long now, he thought.

'Two!'

Tommy groaned. It had been a glancing blow across his left hand, but it counted. The rules meant he would have to walk from now on. There was virtually no chance of avoiding a third and final hit. Not that he particularly cared. A few moments ago he had tried to imagine what wars were like for real, what his brother might be going through at that very moment while Tommy played stupid games in the woods. It had been enough to make him lose his will to win. Tommy slowed his pace until he was almost dawdling. If Fisher was that desperate for victory, good luck to him. As if on cue, his opponent appeared from behind a tree, one meaty fist curled around a cone.

'What's the matter,' Fisher sneered. 'Can't wait to lose?'

'I don't care,' said Tommy. He turned away and set off for the farm. A second later he felt as though he had been stung on the back of his head. Spinning round he saw Fisher bending to reach for something else to throw. 'Don't bother,' he said. 'You've won.' It was not the point. Fisher was only interested in hurting him now. The boy was older than the rest of them and seemed to thrive on bullying. His mates looked up to him, which was how he had become involved in the games. Tommy sighed. It had been so much more fun before Fisher arrived on the scene, but nobody had the nerve to tell him.

'I always win,' Fisher called. 'And I'll win again next week. If you and your useless mates aren't too scared to turn up.'

'We'll turn up,' said Tommy. 'And we'll win.'

'Yeah, yeah. Like you've won every game so far this

year, right? You'd be useless in a real war. Just like your brother.'

Red rage filled Tommy's mind. He took a step forward, then faltered when he saw Fisher's mates emerge from their hiding places. No doubt they were waiting to see how he would react, and join in should he start a fight with the other boy. Well, he was going to disappoint them. No point in starting something he knew he would lose. Besides, he would not have felt like a scrap even if Fisher had been alone. He shook his head and, ignoring the jeers and whistles from behind, walked on towards the ruined farm.

'Don't forget next Sunday, chicken!'

It was Fisher, determined as ever to have the final word. Tommy was tempted to shout something back, but decided it was not worth the effort.

His friends were waiting for him. At least they had the decency to pretend he had only lost them the game through bad luck, though it must have been apparent even from yards away that he had pretty much given up. Tommy didn't really feel like talking to them. Their sympathy, while not cloyingly obvious, still made him uncomfortable. It was better to say nothing, to keep his feelings locked away. When they asked him about the next weekend, and whether they would take up Fisher's challenge, he simply told them he would be there.

Then he went home.

★

It was nearly six o'clock. Cooking smells filled the house. The windows were open but the air was heavy, and so still it felt dead. Evening would soon draw in. This was Tommy's favourite time of day. He liked to sit by his bedroom window and watch the setting sun touch the tall treetops, igniting them. Perhaps tonight, though, he would stay downstairs with his parents. He felt as if he should.

He sighed and lay back on his bed, trying to concentrate on the adventure novel he had borrowed from the library. When he realized he was reading the same lines over and over again he gave up. Not even the laughter of children playing in the streets could raise his spirits. If anything, it only deepened his mood, made him feel more isolated than ever.

Tommy wished he could talk to someone who understood how he felt. Not one of his friends. They were too young to really grasp what was happening in Bosnia. Apart from that, they were probably not particularly interested. The war had not affected their lives the way it had Tommy's.

What made it worse was the fact that Jane, his older sister, was not around to comfort him any more. She had wanted to come home when Tommy's parents told her the news about Michael, but they had insisted she should stay in Cambridge. It was her first year in university and Mum and Dad had argued that her studies must take priority. Jane had only agreed after making them promise to contact her as soon as they heard anything.

Which left Tommy alone. It was not a pleasant feeling.

He heard his mother calling him down for dinner. Meal times were usually quite light-hearted affairs in their house. For the last few days, though, Tommy's parents had almost looked on eating as something they had to do simply to keep going. Nothing more. There was no pleasure in it. Neither of them talked about anything other than the war, and they demanded absolute silence the moment the TV news started. Whenever the telephone rang they almost jumped out of their seats.

You couldn't really blame them, Tommy thought.

He went downstairs.

Dad had already started eating. A brief nod was the only sign that he knew Tommy had entered the room. The television was on, its sound turned down. All Tommy could hear was the soft ticking of the clock and the clink of cutlery on china.

He watched his father pick at his food. At least it saved him having to stare at the reminders of Michael dotted around the room. Taking pride of place on top of the television was a colour photograph of him in uniform. Elsewhere were more informal snapshots: Michael in snow gear; in T-shirt and shorts surrounded by a crowd of Kenyan children; with a group of his friends, all smiles and thumbs-up, the rolling green hills of Northern Ireland behind them.

Tommy remembered what it had been like when his brother served his two years in Belfast. His parents had been anxious enough then, but they had seemed to accept the danger as a part of Michael's job. Not so when the Royal Welch Fusiliers were sent to Bosnia to join the United Nations peacekeeping force. 'It's not our problem,' Dad had insisted at the time. 'Why on earth should our boys be put at risk for a country we've never had anything to do with?'

It was a view he had expressed often, and in the end he was proved right. Michael had been helping to man an observation post when the Serbs attacked. They had taken thirty-three soldiers hostage, and talks were under way in an attempt to secure their release. That was all Tommy knew. He did not understand what the fighting was all about, had not even heard of the place where Michael and the others were being held.

It seemed unreal, like some outer space battle in a science fiction film. Except they had seen Michael and the other soldiers on the television, playing cards and laughing as though nothing was wrong. The film had been made by their captors, who so far had resisted all arguments to release them. Mum had cried when she saw it.

'Eat your food, love.'

Tommy blinked. He had not noticed her placing his meal on the table. Although he did not feel much like eating, he supposed he had to try. Wasting it would be wrong. In his letters home Michael had described the food and water shortages. The soldiers would have gone hungry had it not been for the generosity of the people they were protecting, who gave them basic supplies, mostly grains and vegetables, in return.

An hour or so passed. Mum and Dad chatted to him, asked what he had been up to that afternoon. Telling them about the war game did not feel right. He worried it would suggest that he was making light of what had happened to Michael. Instead he simply said he and his friends had been playing in the woods. It was not quite the truth, not quite a lie. Not that it mattered. Tommy realized his parents were only half listening to him.

By nine thirty he was lying on his bed, once again trying to read. It was almost dark. He could still hear children outside, despite the hour. There was a gentle tapping on his bedroom door and Tommy sat up, heart suddenly pounding. Must be news from Bosnia, he thought, only to realize he would have heard the telephone ring had anything happened.

The door swung open and Mum came in, holding a glass of milk. 'I thought you'd like this,' she said. She handed it to Tommy, then sat on the edge of his bed. 'Are you feeling all right? You didn't seem quite your normal self earlier.'

Tommy shrugged. 'I'm OK.'

'Thinking about Michael?'

'Yes,' he said, and sighed. 'All the time.'

'Try not to worry,' said Mum, patting him on the knee.

'I can't help it,' Tommy said. It was the first time either of his parents had asked him how *he* felt about Michael's capture. Not that he held that against them. One of their sons was at home, safe, the other was being held prisoner in a country ripped apart by war. People were dying, adults and children alike. According to the TV reporters, the United Nations captives were not considered to be in danger. Even so, it was only natural their families would fear for their safety.

'Your brother can look after himself,' Mum assured him. 'Soldiers are very well trained, you know. Especially in the Royal Welch.'

Tommy smiled, a little sadly. 'That's what Michael always says. He reckons the best soldiers in the world are British, and the best British soldiers are the Fusiliers.'

'Exactly,' said Mum, straightening up from the bed. 'Now you stop worrying and go to sleep as soon as you've finished your milk. School tomorrow, don't forget.'

She kissed him on the forehead and left Tommy alone with his thoughts. Sleep would not be easily found. It never was on Sundays, when Tommy's mind whirled with thoughts of classrooms, teachers and homework. Robbie Fisher's challenge was something else to worry about. Maybe it would be better not to turn up, Tommy thought, before realizing that would not help him at all. Fisher would make him suffer in some other way, probably by spreading the word that he was a coward.

He could live with that, even if it was not true. What bothered Tommy about ignoring the challenge was that he would be letting his friends down. That was something his brother simply would not do. 'Look after your mates and they'll look after you,' was the way Michael always put it. 'You never know when you're going to need them.'

Fisher was five–nil ahead in the series. Catching up was not the issue at stake. If Tommy could captain his friends to just one victory it would, he hoped, show they were not afraid of the enemy leader and his bullying ways. Tommy nodded, decision made.

He lay awake for a very long time afterwards. Even when he eventually drifted off, his sleep was restless and haunted. He dreamt he was Michael who in turn was dreaming of Tommy, back home. Fact became fantasy. The war games were real. Pine cones were bullets, and they could kill. Around him were explosions while, from somewhere distant, came a ceaseless ringing. Tommy surfaced briefly from sleep, for a moment convinced he had heard the telephone, silenced by his father's voice. Too tired to get out of bed he closed his eyes and returned to the Bosnian forest.

The heat was so intense it almost stole the breath from his lungs. The rifle in his hands was empty but he kept a tight grip on it anyway. He paused for a moment at the edge of a clearing while he worked out his next move. Crossing the grassy area meant presenting himself as a target the enemy snipers could not miss. Yet by staying still he was playing into their hands. Even now they were probably closing in, poised to strike.

Ahead of him was the ruined farmhouse. Its presence, so near but so impossibly far, was almost a form of torture. His mates would be waiting there for him, silently urging him on, willing him to make it through the woods alive. He knew he could not afford to wait any longer. It was now or never. Taking a deep breath, he began to run straight across the clearing, the quickest route as well as the most dangerous.

A sniper emerged from behind one of the trees to his left.

Tommy did not see the bullet, though he heard it strike the ground just behind him. He picked up his pace in an attempt to outrun the sniper, who kept up with him effortlessly. The searing heat took its toll. It would only be minutes before Tommy's tired legs gave up on him.

At that moment the sniper fell, feet entangled in a snake-like cluster of roots. Tommy heard the thump as the soldier hit the hard forest floor. Keep going, a part of his mind shouted. Get to safety while you can! Instead he stumbled to a halt, then began to walk back to where the sniper was on his knees, spitting out dirt and leaves. Tommy unslung his rifle and pointed it straight at the enemy's face, before lowering it to the ground.

'You lost,' he said calmly.

Fisher stood. His angry face was streaked with grime. There was a long scratch on his left arm and his jeans were torn. He glared at Tommy, then picked up the pine cone he had dropped when he fell. 'Oh yeah?' he said. His arm whipped forward and the cone was suddenly rushing towards Tommy, who saw it as though in slow-motion and deftly side-stepped it.

'You lost,' Tommy repeated, and suddenly laughed. 'Nothing can touch me!'

He spun round and sprinted for the farmhouse, feeling lighter than air.

Nearly home, he thought. Nearly home.

Two brothers, both nearly home.

THE CHRISTMAS TREE

By Linda Newbery

'We'll decorate the tree today. You can help me when you come back from your lessons. Would you like that?' Eva's mother said at breakfast.

Eva said, 'Yes, please,' trying to match her mother's enthusiasm. Her father, hidden behind the pages of *The Times*, showed no sign of having heard. Decorating the Christmas tree had always been a treat: arranging it in its tub in the entrance hall, decking its branches with tinsel and painted baubles and the little candle-holders, and finally hanging the wrapped gifts from its lower branches.

There would be fewer presents this year. Last Christmas Eva had had two brothers, even though one of them had been away from home, in the army. This year she had one, and she wasn't allowed to count him as one of the family any more. He hadn't come home since the argument with Father – there had been many arguments, but Eva thought of this one as *the* argument, the final one. Father would not allow Will's name to be mentioned in the house, but Eva and her mother talked about him sometimes, wondering whether Will would find a way to write to them and how soon he would be going over to France. Mother was always sad-eyed and quiet, these days. She would have sided with Will, if her opinion had been asked.

Eva went upstairs to wash her hands and brush her hair, passing the room that was Geoffrey's, still kept ready with all his clothes in the wardrobe, his shoes cleaned and his books on the shelves. Next was the room that had been Will's, which had been cleared out and turned into an extra guest room. Father had made the servants pack up everything Will hadn't taken with him and send it round to his lodgings.

It was the wrong way round: a room kept waiting for the dead brother, no room at all for the living one. But neither of them would ever come back.

Neat and ready, Eva went downstairs for her coat and muff. It was cold in the house, with no fires lit until the afternoon, except in Father's study and in the kitchen. Outside it was colder still; there had been a sharp frost overnight, and every blade of grass was stiffly outlined in white. Eva's breath made clouds as she walked briskly down the front path and shut the gate behind her. There was a chaffinch in the cherry tree, the pink plumage of its breast warm against the whitened twigs, the only living thing in a frozen scene. Will would have noticed that.

Eva wondered whether there would be snow before Christmas. There might be snowball fights and sledging on the hill . . . and then she reminded herself that she was twelve now, and that it was unfair to wish for snow when Will would very likely have to camp out in it.

She turned in at the vicarage gate. There was a wreath of holly at the front door, studded with scarlet berries. Mrs Starkey opened the door to welcome Eva, revealing a large Christmas tree inside, decorated with twists of paper and baubles and carved wooden angels. An advent wreath hung from the ceiling, with three of its four candles already partially melted down.

'Go on up, dear,' Mrs Starkey said.

Eva liked the vicarage better than her own home. It was smaller and not so grand, but warmer, filled with voices and busyness. Upstairs, in the schoolroom, the two children, Edwin and Clarissa, were already seated at their desks, with Miss Glover writing something in French on the blackboard.

'Good morning, Eva,' Miss Glover said. 'Come and warm yourself. We're continuing with our translation.'

'Did you see our tree?' Edwin whispered, and Eva

nodded, hanging her coat and muff on the stand and taking her place at her own wooden desk.

Miss Glover was younger and much nicer than the teacher at the school in town. Whenever Eva saw the children playing outside or being led out on a walk and thought that she might have preferred going to a proper school, she remembered the compensations of having Miss Jessica Glover to teach her French, mathematics, Latin and nature study, and of sharing her lessons with Edwin and Clarissa. Edwin was only twelve, but by far the cleverest of the three, especially at mathematics. He suffered from bronchitis and was too frail for the rough-and-tumble of school life, but his weak body was balanced by a quick, active mind. Bent over his books, his eyes alert, a lock of dark hair flopping over his forehead, he would finish his work far more quickly than the girls, and would often ask Miss Glover questions she couldn't answer.

At the end of morning lessons Miss Glover called Eva back when the other two went downstairs for their midday meal. 'Have you heard from your brother?' she asked.

Eva shook her head.

'I thought maybe you didn't know,' Miss Glover said. 'I had a letter this morning. His battalion will be here tomorrow, at the station. They're leaving for France in the evening.'

Eva stared. 'Oh. But I didn't know you . . .'

'Will and I have been writing to each other since he went away.' The young governess's eyes met Eva's briefly, then her eyes dropped and her pale skin flushed. For a moment Eva felt cheated. Will had been writing to Miss Glover, but not to her! Then she remembered that Will could not possibly have written to her, since Father would not allow it; Father would tear up any envelope addressed in Will's handwriting. Perhaps Will had tried . . .

'He asked me to tell you,' Miss Glover said. 'About tomorrow, I mean. There was no other way. I suppose . . . your father wouldn't want to know . . . wouldn't want to go to the station to see him off?'

'No,' Eva said bleakly. 'We're not allowed to mention his name at home. It's as if Will were dead.'

The abrupt word dropped into the still room like a stone into a pool, sending out slow ripples. Then Miss Glover sighed. 'I know. You'd think, with one son killed, your father would be more forgiving to the other . . .' She pulled herself up. 'I'm sorry. It's not for me to criticize.'

Eva remembered conversations she had overheard, standing in the corridor outside her father's study. Arguments, always arguments. Her father and Will, both angry. Her mother pleading: 'But Gerald, how can you turn him away? He's our only son now. Does that mean nothing to you?'

And the curt reply: 'He's no son of mine. Not now.'

Now Will was going away to the war and her father might never see him again. But Father didn't care. His pride was more important.

'What shall we do about tomorrow?' Eva said. 'What time train is it? Can we go?'

Miss Glover looked relieved, and Eva realized that this was what she had been about to suggest. 'Yes. Will asked me. I'll tell Clarissa and Edwin not to say anything to your father if they should happen to see him at church. We'll say we're going for an afternoon walk.'

They went downstairs and Eva ate her meal in silence, thinking about Miss Glover's news. Will was going out to fight in France, as she had known he would, but it seemed a shock nevertheless to realize that he could be in the trenches by Christmas. At least she would see him, even if only for a minute or two; she would be able to give him his Christmas present. And then there was the even more surprising news that Miss Glover and Will had been writing letters to each other. That meant they were fond of each other; perhaps they loved each other and wanted to get married. She remembered seeing them talking together in the churchyard one Sunday morning; there had been other people around, gossiping as they always did after church, but somehow Will and Miss Glover had seemed to be alone, talking very intently, standing close to each other. She hadn't thought much about it at the time, but now it occurred to her that this was another of the things Father wouldn't like. He would probably have wanted Will to marry someone with money, like Cynthia Bagnold with the long face and the tittering laugh who was always being invited to dinner. But Will would make up his own mind. Miss Glover didn't live in a smart house with servants. She lived with her widowed mother in a cottage near the Post Office, and besides her teaching she worked as a nurse at the Red Cross Hospital at weekends, often doing night shifts. Eva looked at Miss Glover with a new interest. She sat at the far end of the table, talking to Reverend and Mrs Starkey about the plans for a Christmas party in the church hall for convalescent soldiers. Eva saw her for the first time not as a kindly and efficient governess but as an attractive young woman – as Will would see her. She must, Eva estimated, be about twenty-one or twenty-two, nearly the same age as Will; she was slender, with expressive hazel eyes and soft brown hair pinned into a bun, a few strands escaping. Yes, Eva thought, Miss Glover would be a good match for gentle, unassuming Will.

'. . . and then we'll need help to fill the soldiers' stockings with fruit and nuts,' Mrs Starkey was saying.

Everything, even Christmas, revolved around the war these days. Eva could hardly remember a time when the cobbled main street had not echoed to the tramping boots of soldiers as they marched from the training camp at Coldharbour Farm to the shooting range on the common, or to the barracks fifteen miles away. It would be the third Christmas of the war. Eva remembered hearing about the first Christmas Day, when the fighting had stopped, and British and German soldiers had met in No Man's Land to swap cigarettes and photographs. It made it almost seem worse that the two sides went straight back to their job of killing each other as soon as Christmas was over.

Once, when Geoffrey was home on leave, she asked him what it was like to be a soldier.

'You get used to it,' he said. 'It's a job, like any other job, after a while.'

But you didn't get killed doing other jobs. Geoffrey had been killed in January, not in a great battle but leading a wiring party at a place called Fricourt. Eva could clearly remember the awful finality of the telegram, and then, a few days later, a letter from another lieutenant in Geoffrey's company, saying how sorry he was and what a good officer Geoffrey had been. Eva had read and re-read the letter until she almost felt more sorry for this unknown Lieutenant Edward Sidgwick, for having to write it, than she did for Geoffrey. She had never been very close to Geoffrey; he wasn't like Will. Geoffrey, fourteen years older than Eva, had always seemed grown-up, more like an uncle than a brother.

He was like their father. Geoffrey had never argued with Father, never stood up for opinions of his own. He had worked in the family printing business until the war came, and had joined the army as soon as the recruiting posters went up.

Not like Will.

That afternoon, standing on a chair beside the Christmas tree while her mother passed up lengths of tinsel, Eva wondered whether to say anything about Will leaving for France. Her father was safely out of the way, at work, not due home for another two hours. Several times she opened her mouth to speak and then found herself saying something unimportant instead. She would tell her mother afterwards, she decided. Knowing that Will was so close, at the railway station, would only make her mother miserable; she would never dare to disobey Father's orders by going to see him off. Or she might even tell Father and, if he found out, *no*-one would be allowed to go. No, Eva decided, it was really Miss Glover's secret, not to be told.

She wired the gauze-clad angel to the top of the tree and looked down at her mother. 'How does that look?'

'That's perfect, darling. Thank you. We'll wait and light the candles when your father gets in.'

Eva got down from the chair, suddenly feeling older and wiser than her mother. Mother still thought that the emptiness in the house could be filled by Christmas-tree candles, that a few tiny flames could thaw the icy coldness at its heart. Father was just as illogical: for some reason he had bought an unusually large tree this year, so tall that its leading shoot almost touched the ceiling, as if he thought that the extra shilling or two he had spent could make up for everything else that was lacking. Why should one person have the right to make three others unhappy? She didn't understand. It would have made more sense if her father had left home and Will had stayed.

Her mother went into the drawing room, and Eva stood for a moment looking at the tree. She would fetch down her wrapped gifts later, but Will's present would have to stay hidden. She glanced along the corridor towards her father's study door, where she had listened so often that she could almost see a shadowy ghost of herself crouched by the keyhole. The whole house seemed to stand and wait whenever Will and her father had a 'private talk'. There had been so many quarrels, starting with Will's choice of career.

'You want to be a *journalist*?' Father had sneered. 'A reporter for some cheap newspaper? When there's a job waiting for you in the family business?'

Then Will's voice, calm and determined. 'I don't want a ready-made job, Father. I want to make my own way.'

A loud *hmmph* of protest. 'In my day you'd have

been grateful for the chance. You want to turn your back on everything I've worked for, everything I've built up for you and Geoffrey. You try making a living for yourself out of journalism, boy, and you'll find it's not quite so easy as you think. You'll soon come to me begging for a job . . .'

Then, when Will had insisted, and the dispute had frozen into chilly silence, war had broken out. Will had refused to enlist, in spite of Geoffrey's example. His father had been furious, calling him a coward, ignoring Will's insistence that he was acting on principle. By the October of 1914 Will had packed his bags and moved out to lodgings in town.

And now that Will *was* a soldier, Father still wasn't satisfied. Conscription had come, and Will had returned to tell Father that he had been called up and was going away to training camp. That had caused the final row. Eva found this hard to understand. Father had wanted Will to be in the army. Did it make so much difference whether he was an officer or a private soldier?

Father thought so. 'A son of *mine*, in the rank and file! After all I've worked for, to give you an education, a decent upbringing!' Listening, terrified, Eva could picture her father leaning over his desk, his thick eyebrows drawn low in fury; Will standing very straight, refusing to give way.

Will's voice was quiet. 'You know how I feel about

war, Father. If you don't understand, it's not because I haven't done my best to explain. You can only see it as cowardice. I am joining up because the law of the land says I must. But I refuse to be an officer. I won't order other men to do what I can't believe in myself.'

'You are insolent.' Her father's voice was so loud now that Eva stepped back from the door, fearing that he was about to burst out. 'This is your idea of gratitude, I suppose, to throw this in my face? You, a private soldier, along with every farmhand and factory boy and shirker? How am I to hold my head up, when all my acquaintances have sons who are lieutenants, even captains? When Geoffrey died proudly for his king and country?'

Eva listened to the awful silence that followed. Her father's voice had sounded almost strangled, as if he might burst into tears. And then quick heavy footsteps crossed the floor and Eva scuttled away quickly to hide in the shadows of the staircase. The study door crashed open, and her father's final words were flung into the entrance hall. 'Don't expect to be admitted to this house again. There's no place for you here.'

'Very well, Father.' Will's back was to Eva as he emerged from the study, but she could see that he was in soldier's uniform. She would have run after him, but her father stood there blocking the way until Will had replaced his cap and let himself out of the front door. She could hear Father breathing hard. Then he went slowly back into his study and shut the door.

And that was the last time she had seen Will. But tomorrow she would see him again. She turned over her secret knowledge from time to time, like a child fingering the presents by the Christmas tree.

Next day the frost was hard and sharp again. Eva fidgeted through her lessons, unable to discipline her mind to the study of algebra and French irregular verbs. Once she looked up and caught Miss Glover's eye, and knew that they were both edgy and impatient, willing the hours to pass.

Eva could hardly eat her mutton and boiled potatoes at the midday meal. At last it was time for the afternoon walk. Miss Glover, the two girls and Edwin set off across the fields to follow the footpaths along the river and back by the station. Eva shivered as the cold air bit at her face; the afternoon already had the chill of night-time. It was the shortest day of the year, and the sun was sinking as if drawn down by its own weight, a flaming orb against the winter trees. It threw its dying light across the winter landscape, so that the tips of the alder trees by the river were lit with a reddish gleam against the frosted fields behind. The misted air held the light, heavy and glowing. Birds sheltering in the hawthorns flew away chacking as the group approached, and Eva saw the pale flash of their underwings.

'Thrushes,' Clarissa said, and Miss Glover quickly corrected her, 'No, fieldfares.'

Eva wondered whether Miss Glover and Will had walked together in these fields watching the fieldfares sheltering in the shrubs. Usually, in spite of the cold, Eva would have dawdled to watch the birds. Today she was nervous and fidgety, in case they arrived at the station too late. Miss Glover, too, was setting a brisker pace than usual. They hurried down the slope towards the cluster of railway buildings. The train was already there, waiting in a pall of steam as if huddling into a warm cloak against the chill. Its carriages were empty.

'We're in time,' Miss Glover said. She handed Clarissa some coins. 'Here. This is for the ribbon I asked for,' she said, and Clarissa and Edwin went off obediently along the main street. Eva and Miss Glover waited outside the station.

At the beginning of the war, soldiers marching to the station would have drawn crowds to cheer and wave. By now the sight was commonplace, and on such a cold afternoon as this only a few people came from their homes or their businesses. Eva heard the *tramp, tramp* of soldiers' boots before she could see anyone; then the column rounded the corner by the Post Office, led by an officer on horseback. There were dozens and dozens of men in khaki, marching in step. Her heart sank. Even if she saw Will, he wouldn't be allowed to break rank.

She clutched at Miss Glover's sleeve. 'How will we find him?'

Miss Glover was scanning the rows of faces. 'He'll be looking out for us.'

The officer dismounted and gave his horse's reins to the station boy, told the men to fall out and went through to the station master's office. Eva wondered whether the horse was going on the train too, and then on the boat to France. The soldiers crowded up, easing their packs from their shoulders, some taking out cigarettes. Eva was engulfed in a surge of male bodies, smelling of khaki and sweat and tobacco. She noticed how young some of the soldiers were – when she thought of soldiers, she thought of full-grown men, strong and brave, but some of these were only boys, with slim shoulders and smooth faces. And then suddenly Will was there beside her, dumping his pack on the ground.

'You came, then – I'm so glad . . .' He hugged her quickly and kissed her cheek, and then he hugged Miss Glover too. His face was thin and serious, shadowed beneath the clumsy peaked cap. His hair was cut very short, much shorter than when Eva had last seen him.

'Oh, *Will* – we had to see you, even if it's only for a minute or two . . . !' Eva didn't want to let go of him. It seemed impossible that he could be here, solid and real, and in a few minutes' time he would be gone. He was going Over There, to face all that Over There meant.

And then, ridiculously, even though they had only a few precious minutes to spend together, it was impossible to think of anything to say. There was so much.

'Well, I . . . I'll write,' Will said. Eva supposed he meant he would write to Miss Glover.

'And we'll write to you, won't we, Eva?' Miss Glover said, and then, looking up at him intently, 'Take care of yourself, Will.'

'I will,' he promised, and they all stood there in silence for a moment, realizing, Eva thought, what a meaningless thing it was to say. How could anyone take care of himself, Over There? The soldiers around him were starting to pick up their packs and funnel slowly through the station gates.

Will looked at Eva. 'I suppose Father . . . ?'

'He doesn't know you're going today,' Eva said. 'Or that we came to see you. He wouldn't have—'

'No, I suppose not,' Will said. And then someone jostled him and said, 'Come on, mate,' and he said reluctantly, 'Well, I must get on the train. Take care.' Eva remembered the fountain pen which she had wrapped up for his Christmas present, and she pressed it into his hand. He hugged and kissed her again, and then he kissed Miss Glover as well and whispered something to her which Eva couldn't hear. And then he shouldered his pack and followed the other soldiers

through to the platform, not turning round, but raising a hand in farewell. Neither Eva nor Miss Glover spoke, but they stood waiting until the train pulled slowly away from the platform. Miss Glover's eyes were all wet and shiny.

Eva sent a silent prayer after Will. He hadn't wanted to go to war, but now he was going. And Geoffrey hadn't come back. She thought of her father's voice saying, 'Geoffrey died proudly for his king and country.' Will didn't want to die proudly. He didn't even want to fight. He was only going because of conscription, which meant he would be sent to prison otherwise.

'My father says he's a coward.' She had blurted it out without meaning to.

'Of course he isn't.' Miss Glover spoke with a fierceness that surprised Eva. 'It took courage to stand up to your father. It takes courage to stand up for what you believe in. It's much easier to do what you're told, to let other people decide for you. If he was a coward he would have done what your father wanted all his life. He isn't a coward, Eva – don't let anyone tell you he is.'

Eva wanted her to say more, but Clarissa and Edwin rejoined them and they walked back home in the twilight without discussing Will further.

Later, while she walked the short distance between the vicarage and home, Eva thought about what Miss

Glover had said. Perhaps Father had got it wrong: Will was braver than Geoffrey, after all, even though Geoffrey had enlisted straight away. Geoffrey had simply done what was expected of him, unquestioning. She walked slowly, not wanting to get home just yet, her mind full of the sadness of parting, but at the same time thrilling to the realization of what it was like to be in love. She had seen, for the first time, the glamour and hopelessness and joy of it, the way Miss Glover had looked at Will, not saying anything at all because there was so much to say, and she had seen Will whisper something to her for no-one else to hear. They were in love. Eva had always thought of the phrase in connection with the silly stories the servants read. Now she had seen what it meant.

Indoors, the thick curtains were drawn to block out the light and the Christmas tree stood in splendour, its candles lit. It was a mockery, a failed attempt to bring warmth to the loveless house.

At dinner Eva watched her father eating, opening his mouth to receive chops, potatoes, greens from the kitchen garden, and then snapping it shut. He chewed in a precise, fussy way, tight-lipped, as if wanting to find fault. Eva thought, I don't even like my father. He's my father but I don't even like him, let alone love him. Why should he tell me what to think?

Summoning up her courage, she said boldly, 'Will's

battalion left for France today. I went to the station and saw him.'

She heard her mother's sharp intake of breath. Father paused, a loaded fork halfway to his mouth. Then he replaced the food on his plate and said quietly, 'You know quite well, Eva, that I will not have William's name mentioned in this house.'

'But I have mentioned it.' Eva could feel her limbs trembling.

'Eva, please!' Her mother looked at her with wide, anxious eyes.

'Will is my brother. *I* haven't quarrelled with him,' Eva said. She heard the quiet determination in her voice, as if it were Will speaking. But no, it was her own voice.

'I will not be defied like this!' Father pushed his plate away and stood up, leaning over the table. His lower jaw jutted. 'Go to your room, Eva.'

Her courage gave way. 'Very well,' she said, putting down her knife and fork and standing too. 'But I will go upstairs and think about Will. No-one can stop me doing that.'

She closed the door behind her and went upstairs. It was so cold that she decided to get undressed and go straight to bed. She was still hungry, but she knew Mother would get the housekeeper to smuggle some milk or biscuits and cake up to her soon. Tomorrow she would tell Miss Glover what had happened. And now, she would start a letter to Will, a long one, to say all the things there hadn't been time to say at the station.

Before long she heard the dining-room door open, and her father's stumpy footsteps crossing the hall and going into his study. She knew that he would shut himself up for the rest of the evening, drinking port and smoking cigars.

He would brood there, sullen and angry, in the bitter solitude he had created for himself. For a brief moment Eva felt sorry for him.

HENRY'S HALL
by Robert Leeson

My friend Harry was a snob, just like his dad and his mum. When she was around you had to call him Henry. Which is one reason why we hardly ever went round to his house. I wouldn't have gone there at all, but he had a younger sister called Alice. She was so different, it almost makes you believe those stories about babies being swapped over in their cradles.

Yes, Harry was a snob. So why did Dobbo (Jimmy Dobson) and I put up with him? Well, one reason was he could fight both of us – separately or together – with one hand tied behind his back. And he could fight pretty well anybody in the gang round the corner. So what he said went, more or less.

Now on Saturdays, his idea of a thrill was to go out

over the moor to a place called Marcroft Hall. It was a big, yellow stone house in its own grounds, as old as the hills, one of the ruins Cromwell missed out on when he was breaking the other places up.

Around the Hall was a big park, with dark green bushes that dripped when it rained. Dobbo and I thought it was a creepy hole. But Harry thought it was marvellous.

The squire up at the Hall had gamekeepers with shotguns. They were reckoned to shoot on sight if you put your big toe over the fence.

But Harry would say, as if he'd had this brilliant idea: 'Let's go over to t'Hall.' Dobbo and I would mutter and grumble but in the end we went, for want of anything better to do. Alice would come with us, if she could get away. Their mother thought it wasn't nice, a girl going out with boys in the woods and that.

We'd walk over the moor, sneak through the park and get right up to the wall and the big iron gate. A gravel drive led up to the main door. Harry would look at it, mouth open, while Alice shrugged her shoulders and Dobbo and I winked at each other.

'They used to have a coach and six here,' said Harry, 'when they had a big ball or a party.'

'That's nowt. We had a coach and thirty on the outing to New Brighton last year,' said Dobbo.

'You ignorant pig,' spluttered Harry. 'I mean a coach

and six horses. They lived in style, then. I mean, look at that garden – they must have a small army of men looking after that – as well as grooms and footmen and parlourmaids, and—'

'Hey up,' interrupted Dobbo, suddenly pointing. 'Look at that!'

We looked. Right at the end of the garden, on a sort of little platform, was the statue of a woman – with nothing on.

'D'you reckon that's his missis?' went on Dobbo.

Alice and I hid our faces. Harry blew up. 'You're disgusting, Dobbo. You've got a one-track mind.'

I changed the subject quickly. 'Well, you won't get inside there, Harry, unless your dad buys it.'

Harry took the bait like a hungry perch. 'He might do that, an' all.'

Alice rolled her eyes. She was always embarrassed when her brother went on like this. Harry wasn't stopping there, though. 'Yeah, he might yet. But not before the old squire goes . . . that wouldn't be right.'

It was too much. Dobbo and I rolled over on the grass laughing ourselves sick. 'Oh my,' mocked Dobbo. 'Your dad wouldn't be such a rotten cad, driving the old squire out, would he?'

The penny dropped for Harry. He lost his rag and went for us, fists and feet going at once. Between clouts he yelled: 'You wait . . . (*thump, thump*) . . . I'll be living in that Hall . . . (*thump, thump*) . . . you'll (*thump*) see.'

121

Alice came and pulled Harry off Dobbo and me before he pulverized us. Dobbo didn't give up, though. 'You, in the Hall? I should coco. How much d'you bet?'

'Five quid,' said Harry. He must have been mad. Our eyes shot out of our heads – three or four years' pocket money.

It nearly silenced Dobbo. But not quite. 'You're on,' he said.

Summer came. We had other things to think about, like starting the big school in the autumn. But there were bigger changes, from further away, coming to our lives.

One hot day we went over to the Hall again. As we came down from the ridge overlooking Marcroft Park, we stopped and stared at one another. Great brown patches showed where the green turf had been torn up. Great grey steel gun barrels pointed to the sky.

Dobbo chuckled. 'The old squire's not going without a fight, Harry.'

Harry snorted. He always had problems seeing a joke – especially where the Hall was concerned.

'Those guns are to keep Hitler out. There's going to be a war, come Christmas.'

'Get off,' said Dobbo. 'Dad says there won't be a war. Our side's too strong.' He ticked off on his hands.

'There's Britain, France, Holland . . . and Russia . . . then there's America.'

'I don't know,' I put in. 'My dad reckons we'll have to fight Hitler.'

My dad was right. Dobbo's was wrong. War came. When we saw the Hall again, barbed wire blocked the path. The ack-ack guns had gone. In their place were rows of trucks with greeny camouflage paint.

Dobbo pointed. 'Squire's got the removal vans in. Run home and tell your dad.'

But none of us laughed. War was getting closer, more real every day. From the ridge we could see in the distance the barrage balloons, like grey airships, forming a ring round Liverpool to keep enemy planes out.

Then the coaches started to arrive in our village, bringing the evacuees, pale-faced, tough-looking, miserable kids from the cities. They were supposed to be brought to our place for safety. But most of 'em couldn't wait to go back home, bombs or no bombs.

Every day when we went to school, we had to carry our gas masks and our blue identity cards.

As the year turned, the news was worse. Hitler's armies were tramping over everywhere. And Mussolini in Italy joined in on his side.

It was early summer when we saw the park again. Now the grass was covered with brown and white tents. Tired men in dirty khaki lay half-asleep in the sun.

'Those are our soldiers, just been brought back from France,' Dobbo told us. For some reason he was whispering.

'My dad reckons some of them are going off again to fight right away,' I answered.

'It's not right. Wish I was old enough. I'd go instead.'

There was no answer to that. We looked at the exhausted men on the grass. They looked back without a word.

Alice said: 'We shouldn't stare. Come on.'

We trailed away. Harry hadn't opened his mouth.

The soldiers marched away. But the war came even closer. We sat on the ridge over the park, but we weren't looking at the Hall. Our eyes were fixed on the blue sky above, criss-crossed with white vapour trails. Far, far away we could hear the sound of aircraft engines – the up-and-down beat of the German bombers, the whine of the Spitfires and Hurricanes as they closed in. Then, suddenly, and seeming very close, the hard sound of machine-gun fire.

'If I were a fighter pilot,' said Harry, 'I'd shoot 'em down like flies, like flies.'

He sliced through the air with his hand, making howling noises. He seemed to have forgotten about the Hall and the old squire. The sounds came closer in the sky, grew louder. Gunfire crackled again.

Suddenly it seemed as if an express train was tearing through a tunnel behind us. We turned and cringed at the same time as a plane dived down, growing huger by the second. Down we fell on the ground, clapping our hands over our ears as the grey bomber with the black crosses vanished beyond the trees.

Harry sprang up. 'One of theirs. He's copped it. Come on. Let's have a look where it comes down.'

We ran down the slope. I could feel my chest go tight with excitement. Dobbo gasped: 'If we get . . . close enough . . . we might get . . . a bit off the wing or an ammunition round. My . . . cousin did, a week back.'

The ground danced under our feet. A great gush of black smoke shot above the trees and then came the explosion. Now the air was full of flying debris, like dark rain.

'Look at that,' yelled Harry, pointing down. 'A chunk off the fuselage.' Then he glared at us. 'That's mine – I saw it first.'

He rushed ahead and, grabbing the dull grey metal with its black markings, held it up in triumph. Then, just as quickly, he let it drop. He turned round, his face grey.

'What's up?' demanded Alice.

'It's got skin and hair and – stuff on it . . .' he whispered.

*

That autumn we were picking potatoes on the farms, collecting waste paper and scrap for the war effort. The Hall was forgotten.

But one winter day when the trees were black and bare, we went back there. The park was full of men in maroon jackets, dark round patches on their backs.

'Those are Eyties,' said Harry, 'Mussolini's men. Prisoners from North Africa. We're winning now.'

'What are those circles on their backs for?' asked Alice.

'Don't you know?' he said scornfully. 'That's for if they run away. The guards have a good mark to shoot at.'

'Shoot them in the back?' asked Alice. 'That's horrible.'

'Get off. There's a war on. They'd do worse to us.'

Sometimes it seemed we were winning. Sometimes not. The war spread to Russia. I got out a map at home and tried to make sense of the names – Rostov, Smolensk, Staganrog. That country was so huge, surely Hitler would never beat them.

I found a picture in a newspaper of Russian partisans fighting behind the German lines. One of them looked no older than me – he was no taller than his rifle.

'D'you think it'll last long enough for us to get into the army?' I asked the others.

Harry's lip curled. 'Army? Get off! I'm going to be

er pilot and bomb Germany flat.'

'My dad says,' remarked Dobbo, 'that they've got too many pilots. They're transferring them all to the Catering Corps.'

Harry's face fell. 'Why?' he asked seriously.

'There's a shortage of kitchen hands. They all died eating their own cooking.'

'I'll thump you, Dobbo,' said Harry. But Dobbo was out of the way, sharpish. I was laughing too much to move. So Harry thumped me, till Alice stopped him.

The Americans moved into Marcroft Park. Monstrous machines chewed up the ground, smashing down trees, digging ditches, laying roads.

'Not much left for your dad to take over, Harry,' said Dobbo.

'They can't have touched the Hall,' said Harry, deep shock in his voice. 'Hey, come on.'

We dodged around the engineers and sneaked up to the wall around the Hall gardens.

But suddenly a man in olive-green uniform stood in our path. His face was black. I'd never seen a black man before. Across his chest he carried a tommy gun. His voice was deep. 'Can't come through here, kids.' But he grinned as he spoke, then fished in his pocket. 'Have some candy.'

Candy? What he handed us was strips of chewing gum. 'Now, move it before the captain comes.'

*

We knew our side was winning. And our lives were changing. Harry was older than the rest of us and left school first. But he didn't get to be a bomber pilot. His mother made sure he went into a 'reserved occupation'. He ended up in an aircraft factory, breaking up bombers, not flying them.

Dobbo went off somewhere to study book-keeping. 'Wish it was book-making,' he told me. But I knew he'd land on his feet, like a cat.

Alice was kept at home 'to help mother'.

I joined the local newspaper as a junior – reporting weddings and funerals and pigeon-fanciers' annual dinners.

But the war was still there. Every now and then they'd let me write a story about a local boy killed in action, or 'missing' on a raid over Germany. I had to go and persuade the mother to let us have her only picture to put in the paper. 'You will let me have it back, won't you?' she said, nearly crying.

'Promise,' I answered, hoping the printers wouldn't let me down and lose it.

The park around the Hall filled up again. This time there were German prisoners of war, in grey-blue uniforms with patches on their backs.

Then they were moved out and other people moved into the Hall – it was turned into a conva-lescent home for our wounded. And that was how I ﬁrst of our gang to get inside the place.

went there to interview a local man, a war hero, a
ommando. I knew it would be good – a real story
about action, raids by night, blowing up German
guns, parachute landings, contacting the Resistance
ﬁghters.

Beyond the stone steps and big front door a broad
staircase opened up. But the steps were bare boards
and there were no pictures on the walls of squires
from olden times. It was all clean and empty and smelt
of disinfectant.

I found the wounded Commando lying on his bed
in a little room with the sunshine coming in through
the window. I swallowed when I saw him. This a war
hero? He was like an old man, thin as a rake in his
blue-striped pyjamas. His voice was as thin and weak
as his body. But he talked.

He'd been captured and sentenced to death; then
he'd escaped, walked halfway across Germany and
been recaptured, sentenced to death again, then sent
to forced labour in a shell factory.

'We were a mixed bag, son – Poles, Russians, Jews,
Serbs. They fed us pig-swill, but they fed us. They
needed us. You think I'm thin,' (he could see me looking at him out of the corner of my eye), 'you should
have seen the others – skin and bone.

'As the Red Army was coming closer, the guards
panicked. Some wanted to march us all westwards, the

others wanted to get rid of us. In the end they decided to pick out the British and the French and march them off. Then they shot the others – got 'em to dig the pits first, then killed them so they fell in. The graves filled up and the bodies piled and piled . . .'

'I took my chance and slipped away one day at dusk. That night the Yanks came over, a thousand-bomber raid, and the nearest town brewed up like a bonfire. They call it a firestorm these days – it turned night into day.

'When I got in there, everything – ruins, bodies – was covered with white ash. Little kids burned to a crisp, their bodies black.'

He stopped and looked up at me. 'Yes, son, I've seen a lot of action – and I've seen a lot of death. But it was mostly civilians – I was lucky to be a soldier. There you are . . . see if they'll print that.'

All the same I joined the army as soon as I could. I found out you could get in at seventeen. The war was over but I wanted to get away.

The army wasn't quite what I'd imagined – more like hard work, square-bashing, assault courses, route marches – half-dead with fatigue, dragged out of bed at dawn, falling back into bed at night. And I was always hungry.

It made me glad to get home on leave. The home town I'd wanted to get out of seemed like heaven to

me – for a few days. And who d'you think I met?
Alice, in her Land Army uniform, khaki shirt, breeches
and a hat like an Australian sheep farmer. She'd got
away from home too, though I don't know how she
did it. She looked smashing, which was more than
I did. My uniform fitted where it touched.

It was a hot summer's day. We walked out over the
moor, out of force of habit. The grounds of the Hall
were full of tin huts, with lines of washing strung
between them. Tired women and thin, pale children
sat outside.

'They're DPs,' said Alice.

'What's that?'

'Displaced Persons. They come from all over. Lost
their homes in the war and can't get back.'

I'd been half thinking of making a joke about Harry
and the Hall, but I changed my mind.

Three years passed before I was home for good in a
civilian suit. It fitted me better than my uniform – just.

As I got off the train, a tall bloke with a thin, blond
moustache, and a broad-brimmed trilby pulled down
over his eyes like a wide-boy, stepped up and said:
'Carry your kit-bag for a tanner, soldier?'

I stared, then laughed. 'Dobbo, you daft oink, where
did you spring from?'

'Oh, I'm often down here, do a lot of business.
Come and have a drink.' He led me into the station
refreshment room.

Looking round at the drab brown walls, he said: 'This'll do for now. But next time I'll treat you up at the new Country Club.' There was a funny look in his eyes.

'Country Club?' I said. 'Never heard of it.'

''Course you haven't. Up at Marcroft Hall. Only just opened. Very posh.'

'I bet it's pricey, too.'

'Dead right,' said Dobbo, still with that funny gleam in his eye. 'Cost me a fiver before I even turned round.'

'I dunno, Dobbo,' I said. 'You can pay five quid for a good round these days.'

He crowed with laughter. 'No, that was *before* the drinks. The new bar manager took it off me as soon as I came in. Said I owed it him.'

Suddenly I understood. 'The manager . . . is that . . .'

'Right first time. Harry. He lives in. Bores the members rigid with stories about the old squire. He's got the old butler's room upstairs. And you know what the regulars call the place? Henry's Hall, that's what.'

THE OPEN WINDOW
by Laurence Staig

Once again it was a night of restless sleep. Jamie awoke
in fits and starts, sweat running down his face like soft
river tributaries. He blinked and wiped away the grit
from his eyes. His cotton pyjamas clung to his body as
though they were a second skin. Every so often the
familiar crackle, followed by the high-pitched scream
and rush from somewhere far off, seemed that much
closer, making him suddenly glance upwards. His
anxious eyes tried to imagine they could see past the
sweep of the fan, which throbbed above him like the
beat of helicopter blades. Jamie tried to peer through
the ceiling itself and into the night sky. He had been
assured that he was safe, but they seemed so near
tonight, they even drowned out the comforting

135

murmuring hum and clickety-click of the insects.

For a moment the door of his bedroom opened slightly and a wide yellow V yawned across the floor, stopping short of his bed. The shadow of his mother stood silent and still, then after a moment he heard her voice. 'Are you all right?'

'Yes,' he found himself saying, raising his head.

'Don't worry, be brave. We'll be out of here by the time the fighting gets this far, if it ever does.'

He lowered his head to the pillow once more. Behind his mother he saw the small round form of Saku.

'Is everything OK, Madam?' He spoke in urgent whispers. 'The boy? Problems?'

'No, no,' his mother said in a hushed, but troubled voice. 'I was just looking in at him.'

'Noisy tonight, Madam. Perhaps another room in the building after tomorrow would be better.'

'No, it's all right. Go to bed, Saku, and thank you.'

She remained in the doorway for a further few minutes, before closing the door. The yellow V dissolved into the night and he was alone once more. A sudden burst of staccato crackle made Jamie open his eyes wide. Through the slats in the shutters came blade-shaped streaks of light, as though outside a demon of blinding intensity was trying to get in. The thud of the fan beat down. He turned over onto his back and stared into the blurry outline. Saku had told him that it could send him to sleep if he concentrated, almost like the swing of a snake charmer's pipe. Outside, the sudden sound of the rain came like the long-awaited arrival of a friend. The pitter-patter of the rain always worked for him. It was as though the heavens had sent a cleansing wash, to clear away the dirt and grime, the blood and crimes of man against man which daily dressed the streets of the city. Its comforting beat joined the sound of the fan and together they drummed him away into dreamland.

Saku opened the shutters wide like a magician revealing the secrets of his magic cabinet. Jamie screwed up his eyes as sunlight streamed in and bathed his pillows in a splash of golden light.

'You sleep in this morning, young sir?'

Jamie pulled himself up and looked about for his clock. His mother had moved it to the top of his near-by dresser. It stood amongst his school photographs, a round face with thick black hands and a large pair of brass bells for a hat. The hands showed 8.15.

Saku saw him peering at the clock. 'You are usually up much earlier and practising the running. Better that you sleep in though – it was madness last night. The meeting place at the edge of the city was hit, but much of the fighting was still at the foothills. Not too much trouble. Not too much . . .'

Saku's voice trailed off as he lost something of his

smile. He picked up one of Jamie's photographs. Within the wooden frame was a photograph of Jamie as he broke through the ribbon at one of his school sports days. It had been taken back in England just before they left. The beaming happy face had been caught perfectly by the camera, the moment he won the 400 metres.

'Some good news, young sir,' said Saku brightly, as he opened the windows wide. The sharp musty scented smells of the embassy gardens rushed into the room as though they had been poured from a flask. Jamie looked up as he threw the bedcovers back.

'We have some melons, good for breakfast, eh? One of my wife's friends managed a special deal, just for you. Alas, food is still difficult here – but fresh melons! Eh? What do you say? We can pretend there is no war at all.'

Jamie smiled. He knew that Saku had probably given a lot to get them, that they had probably clawed in all kinds of special favours just for him. 'Thank you, Saku,' he said.

'You must still stay in now. In the grounds you are safe until they can come and collect you. Your father said I was to remind you. Better to stay in. Mother and father have been called away – I fear you will not be here for much longer. But good for you, eh?'

He understood. Within the walls he was well protected: the war and its atrocities had hardly touched him in comparison to those who lived in the world outside. He knew that there were almost certainly all kinds of sights in the city that his parents did not want him to see. Once, when they had been invited to tea with a friend of the general's, their jeep had been detoured round the northern edge of the city. His mother had told him that there had been little shelling here, that the main conflict was still out in the desert and the foothill villages. But his eyes told him otherwise.

Three floors of a concrete complex had collapsed from the explosion of a nearby shell. The word on the streets was that it had been intended for elsewhere, a rogue shot. Two groups of women stood wailing and crying, their arms held high, fingers outstretched as if desperately reaching out, seeking something – anything. Soldiers were clawing at concrete slabs, their fingers red and torn as dust clouds billowed upwards while masonry fell.

As the jeep passed close by, their driver pointing to the embassy pass that was fixed to the windscreen, Jamie saw the crushed and folded features that stared out at him from a crevice. An arm pointed upwards behind the face; somehow the angle was wrong – clearly the body had been twisted, bent double on itself beneath the weight of the rubble. One of the soldiers had staggered back and yelled something at another. Jamie had to look away as one of the women had stretched her arms wide in an attitude of despair. She had reminded him of a figure in an opera his parents had once taken him to see in the amphitheatre. It had been a Greek tragedy. The singer had worn a half mask, a pale frozen image of anguish. He could not seek out the face of this woman; he knew it would be the same as the one he had seen at the opera, though it would not be a mask – it would be flesh, it would be real.

'I will stay in,' he said quietly as he stared out into the garden.

Saku stopped fussing with the photographs and glanced at him. 'Are you OK – good boy, young sir?'

Jamie turned and was unable to hold back a sigh. 'Yes, thank you. And thank you for the melon. I must have my run first.'

'Of course,' said Saku. 'And when you have finished Saku will have everything nice for you on the veranda! With some special tea, yes?'

He was like an enthusiastic favourite aunt.

Jamie ran because he was good at it and he harboured hopes that perhaps, one day, his hobby would become something more. He had run for as long as he remembered, and since his parents' decision that he should accompany them abroad he had trained in conditions that were tougher than back home. General Shadaz, who had been liaising with the Red Cross and his father, had told him that perseverance and determination was everything. But he must feel the pain. He must train until it hurt. *Feel it.* He remembered his mother showing the General politely but firmly out onto the balcony as he had begun to advise him with ever-growing enthusiasm. But Jamie knew that he was right.

He ran for other reasons too.

Now he ran to exorcize his demons. He ran to rid himself of the sounds he heard and the sights he saw – or glimpsed on the occasions they had travelled outside the grounds since the war. He ran to immerse himself in another place.

The path which circled the embassy fountains was just less than a kilometre, which was the equivalent of running the 400 metres twice. He thought that he might have it in him to be a long-distance runner and badly wanted to run through the city. There were other boys his own age out there: sometimes he longed to challenge them to a race. But the circle would have to do. The scents of the flowers filled his nostrils – they made his head spin and the run became something else, almost an ecstasy. He closed his eyes and scuffed up the dirt. He had left his Walkman in his room; this morning he listened only to the cries of the birds and far-off children. Suddenly, he stopped and opened his eyes.

He was at the tip of the circle, almost at the halfway point. Through the trees he saw a group of workmen.

They had clearly been busy putting up some kind of wire fencing, which stretched across an opening in the huge terracotta coloured garden wall. They had finished and, with pickaxes and shovels across their shoulders, were heading down towards the house. From the sound of their voices they were laughing and joking. Jamie screwed up his eyes and shielded the sun from his face. One of the men saw him and waved – it was Jamshial, the gardener, who spoke a little English.

'Allo, Mister Jamie,' he called. 'Must 'ave been a hit or somethin' from last night. Those devils are coming nearer each day. Nobody get through there though. You leaving soon, I hear – so sorry, but it best, whole city be leaving.'

Jamie brushed his sun-bleached fringe to the side and acknowledged Jamshial with an upturn of his face, something he had watched Saku do. The men disappeared through the cavern of bowing palms.

The earlier cries of children were louder this time. They were excited cries and there was laughter too, something which Jamie had not heard for some time. He pulled a scarf from his back pocket and tied it into a bandanna around his head, then walked towards the gap in the wall, which was now covered in layers of tightly woven mesh. So the fighting was nearer than he thought. He was certain the city was being targeted: the sudden urgency to get them out had been obvious even though his parents had tried their best to conceal it from him.

Jamie stared through the grid. A barrier supported on trestles had been set up around the opening, just like the kind he had seen erected around road works. The men had done a good job – the makeshift fencing had been stapled into the walls. On the other side he saw mounds of brick and stone rubble. But it was what he saw beyond this that interested him most. It was the first time he had been able to see beyond the northern side of the embassy. He had not appreciated that the grounds were so close to the ordinary streets of the city. To the right stood the remains of a sand-coloured house. Planks had been boarded across the windows and doors. Next to this was a bomb site. Fires still burned and some elderly veiled women in black were sorting through a pile of remains nearby. One woman was trying to make some sense out of pieces of a chair.

But almost exactly opposite, centred in a single-storey wall, was a window. It was an unusual shape, comprised of three openings – a central tall column with two smaller ones on either side, like a cross. Below the window were a group of street boys. Three could not have been much older than nine or ten. But there were another two who might have been twelve or thirteen, around Jamie's age. They were busy scuffling excitedly around some kind of activity that

was taking place on the ground in front of the window. Suddenly a huge laugh broke out from somewhere inside the house and a face appeared at the window. Jamie stepped closer to the grid and put his fingers into the mesh. He held on tightly.

The boy looked down at the others and handed them something – it might have been a few coins. The others leapt about as one spat into his hands and rubbed them together. Once again the boy laughed long and loud, and very soon the others joined in with him.

At first Jamie wasn't sure what they were up to, but after a moment he guessed. They had made a rough kind of track in the dust, partitioning the area with some rocks and old pieces of rope. They were holding a race of some sort with some kind of animals. Jamie was fascinated. He watched in silence.

One of the women who had been helping to put the chair together peered over at what the boys were doing and shouted at them. The boy at the window said something and laughed again. The woman raised her hands into the air and gave a cry. After a moment the entire group were joining in the fun; the reprimand turned into a joyous cry. For a matter of minutes all that Jamie could hear was the laughter of the crowd. The boy had the most unusual and infectious laugh he had ever heard. It was huge and warm and real. Almost without his realizing it a grin had spread across his own face. The boys jumped around clapping their hands and patting one another on the back.

Suddenly a boy in a bright yellow shirt saw Jamie. He stopped in his tracks and pointed. For a moment Jamie wasn't sure what he should do next: he might be in some kind of danger. But the boy called to his friends and waved in his direction. Jamie waved back. The boy at the window called over to him, but he could not understand what was said. Jamie shrugged his shoulders and held his arms out. The boy said something to his friend in the yellow shirt, who then ran across the street to the barrier. He stood silently for a moment and smiled at Jamie. 'Engleesh?' said the boy.

Jamie nodded.

'Come, play game, yes?' He gestured for Jamie to join them.

Jamie shook his head and pointed to the mesh. 'Difficult. Not permitted,' he said.

The boy nodded as though he understood and smiled again.

'What game?' Jamie asked, trying to make himself understood with elaborate arm and hand movements.

'Name of game?' said the boy. Jamie nodded. 'It a race. Three scorpia, you say scorpions?' He made a movement with his hands to imitate a scorpion's tail. Now Jamie understood: it was a game he had heard

146

was popular amongst the local street kids. They raced scorpions and made bets. By now a group of men had joined the children. Coins were being tossed into a rag which lay on the window sill. Jamie gazed past them to the boy at the window, who was tapping coins on the sill with the enthusiasm of a bookmaker at a race track. His smile was almost permanent and the others around him laughed and danced. It was almost like a party and it was easy to see who was the centre of attention, the master of ceremonies.

'Your friend, the boy at the window. Very popular!' said Jamie, pointing across the street.

The boy in the yellow shirt shrugged; he did not understand.

'Name of friend?' said Jamie, pointing.

'Ah! My name is Hussan,' said the boy.

'No,' said Jamie. 'The other boy?'

'Oh, he good friend. Make us happy!' said the boy. 'Must go.'

With that, the boy crossed the street. Jamie watched for a while. Away in the distance came the sound of battle, a rumble as if a shell had gone off in the desert. For a moment the group stopped and listened. The boy at the window said something, a man with a grey beard and a walking stick said something back and tossed a coin in with the others. The boy laughed once more and the street party resumed.

From somewhere behind him Jamie heard the

urgent voice of Saku. It was time to return to the house.

Earlier that evening his parents had discussed the possibility of the city coming under siege. General Shadaz had called by to tell them that the Red Cross was on its way. Their only main concern was about gas: one of the neighbouring villages in the foothills had been struck. The general had said that he had seen nothing like it. Jamie's father had spent a whole hour showing him what to do in the event of an attack. The mask had felt heavy and cumbersome, as if a life form was hugging at his face.

That night was quieter. The distant sounds of shelling crackled and spat like fireworks and, despite it being against orders, Jamie had opened the shutters just slightly. He propped himself up on his pillows and watched the lights in the sky. Every so often the sound of the boy's laughter entered his head; it would not leave him. As his eyes closed he found that the boy's face, and his infectious laugh and smile, replaced the usually comforting thud of the ceiling fan. He soon fell asleep.

In the morning Jamie was up early, even earlier than Saku. But Saku's wife, Sharian, was in the kitchen making breakfast. There was still some melon left and she was sharing it with Jamshial.

'You very early Jamie – cannot sleep?' she asked.

'Slept well,' he said. 'Better than for a long time in fact.'

'The talk is that we will all be moved; it coming soon, I think,' said Jamshial.

Jamie nodded and pointed to the box of gas masks which were on the table.

'It will not come to that,' said Sharian.

'Who lives in that house, the one opposite the fence you put up yesterday?'

Jamshial gave Jamie a piece of his melon and said something to Sharian. He did not understand everything Jamie had said. After a moment he nodded. 'Oh yes, family were killed. Big tragedy, from the north, was much fighting.'

'They play racing games, with the scorpions,' said Jamie.

'Good racing games,' said Jamshial. 'I tell the boys how you race. You run good!'

Jamie smiled and reached into his shorts pocket for his scarf. He rolled it into his bandanna. 'Maybe we could have a race,' he said.

Jamshial frowned, but Sharian translated for him. Jamshial's eyes widened with enthusiasm. 'Oh, that would be good, much fun. We make bets, yes? Only if your mother and father say yes, though!'

'OK,' said Jamie. 'You arrange it, yes? But I'd like to race the boy who lives in that house.'

Sharian translated again.

'All will be arranged,' said Jamshial.

Later that morning Jamie made his run round the circle. But once again he stopped at the far end and returned to the fence. The boy was at the window, as before. His round face was smiling with a grin that cracked from ear to ear. The boys had just finished a race and were re-arranging the scorpions with sticks at one end of the track. Two of the old men who had been there yesterday now sat on a makeshift bench constructed out of an old door. Gradually others were joining them, pulling in chairs and old buckets upon which to sit. The boy in the yellow shirt saw Jamie and waved. Jamie made a thumbs-up sign and gripped the mesh eagerly.

Jamshial appeared round the corner of the house with his arm around one of the boys. He nodded at Jamie. It was obvious that the event was being arranged and was causing much excitement.

Suddenly Jamie heard the voice of his father behind him. 'Jamie, I want a word.'

Jamie turned to find his father standing with General Shadaz. The boy's laugh rolled over to them from across the street. Jamie's father laughed too. 'That boy has got a way!' he said. 'Jamie, we might be leaving this evening. I've come to warn you. Make sure you have your things together. Isn't there some race or something? Sharian mentioned that Jamshial is up to some fun before we have to go.'

'Yes,' said Jamie. For a moment he wondered how he felt about the news that they were going. He had just found a friend. 'The boy with the laugh . . .'

'Ah,' said General Shadaz. 'You mean Abbu – a great kid, laughter of courage!'

Jamie wasn't certain what he meant. He looked back across the road. Jamshial started to walk towards them with the boy in the yellow shirt. The boy at the window, Abbu, vanished for a moment and two of the other boys entered the house.

'Do you know,' continued General Shadaz, 'it is said that children laugh three hundred times a day; adults less than thirty?'

For a moment Jamie looked at the general, then he looked across the street again. As though in slow motion Jamshial walked towards them with the boy in the yellow shirt. Jamie felt a tingling in his legs. He caught his breath.

'Here, young Jamie, sir,' called Jamshial. 'Here is your opponent, all are turning out, big bets and much good time, yes?'

'No,' said Jamie. 'There's some mistake. I wanted to race the boy in the house. The boy at the window! Abbu?'

Jamshial stopped short of the fence. His face had fallen. 'But that is not possible. It is Hussan's house. You said boy who has house. Abbu lives nowhere.'

Jamie heard General Shadaz's voice behind him. 'Abbu was very, very brave. Pulled his sister free after the first bomb. But the second ... Ah! My dear Master Jamie, you cannot race with Abbu.'

The slow-motion film returned as Jamie watched in horror. The two other boys carried the boy who had been at the window out through the side door. The two old men made room for him, while another fetched a cushion. Jamie guessed the situation before he saw it: Abbu had no legs. An old vegetable sack was tied around his waist with string. But his face beamed.

For a moment Jamie could not move. His throat felt full, even when the music of the boy's laughter rang out once more from across the street. Without saying a word he turned and ran back along the path which circled the embassy's fountains. As he ran, all that he could think of were the words of General Shadaz: '*You must feel the pain.*'

Jamie ran and he ran. And he ran and he ran until he could run no more.

THE WATCHING PLACE
by Brian Morse

A crow flapped lazily from tree to tree. A squirrel chattered angrily after it.

Younger Bear watched the woods and all that went on in them. The scouting party had gone away through them yesterday before first light, while the owl was still stalking the air above the camp. Wakeful in his sleeping place by the door of the family tepee, Younger Bear had seen them leaving. Hunting parties returning during the past ten days had reported bands of Sioux warriors moving about the plain that lay half a day's journey over the hills. The two scouts should be back soon to tell what they had learnt.

'Of course, it may mean nothing,' Yellow Eagle, the chief, had said when he'd listened to the hunters' complaints. 'How long have we, the Cheyenne, and the Sioux been at peace? Many seasons. It is probably just the younger Sioux warriors showing off. Young men will be young men. The older warriors will make them see sense and calm them down.' All the same Yellow Eagle had thought it best to check on their fierce neighbours' intentions, for the Sioux were many and Younger Bear's tribe were few.

When Younger Bear turned, Yellow Eagle had come out of the door of his tepee. The chief stood looking from one side of the camp to the other. Younger Bear lowered his gaze. When Yellow Eagle gazed into your eyes it felt as if he could see into your heart. The chief's gaze rested a moment on the boy, then he gestured. Younger Bear ran and knelt at the chief's feet.

The chief towered above him. 'I have watched you, Younger Bear. You miss very little that goes on. One day we will make a warrior of you.' Younger Bear held his breath. 'The scouts will be back soon. Whatever the news, I think it is time for you to make a third pair of eyes at the watching place on the hill tonight while the tribe sleeps.' He looked at Younger Bear intently, then nodded that he had nothing else to say.

Younger Bear quickly walked away. He felt elated. Others, some of them older than him, were playing among the tepees. They called. Younger Bear was tempted, then turned away. He'd been chosen, not them. He had a strange feeling, as if suddenly he no longer belonged with the world he'd lived in for so many summers and winters. But neither did he belong with the warriors, not yet. That part of his life was just beginning.

Suddenly he ran towards the family tepee. Tonight he would be a different person. Tonight would begin the long journey it would take to become a warrior.

The sun was two hand's-breadths above the horizon when the scouts returned. They went straight to the chief. Rumours began to spread like wildfire through the camp. The news was bad: the Sioux were on the war path; they had already attacked another Cheyenne village two days' journey away. The news was good: the Sioux braves had returned to camp.

Not that everyone thought the prospect of war bad. Last year's new warriors and the year before's had never seen battle. They wanted war. They had no scalps on their belts. Older people were not so happy, particularly some of the women. Younger Bear's mother would not welcome fighting – her husband, Younger Bear's father, had been killed fighting a marauding Pawnee war band three winters ago. Although she had married again, she had no wish that her new husband and her son (her face had gone pale when Younger Bear had told her what Yellow Eagle had said) should be taken from her. As Younger Bear squatted waiting for the chief and the scouts to re-appear he could hear his mother and step-father arguing.

'Younger Bear!' It was Great Elk, one of the watchers he was to go with. 'Are you ready?' Little Horse, the other watcher, was already standing by the edge of the trees.

'But Yellow Eagle has not yet told us—'

'They will be discussing all night and all tomorrow,' Great Elk said. He was one of the older warriors, a man to whom many turned for advice. He'd been a friend of Younger Bear's dead father. 'The Sioux are arguing among themselves. I know them. They will settle down. They will not bother us this summer.'

'You have not heard what the scouts say,' Younger Bear said.

Great Elk gave him a hard look for his cheek. 'I saw their faces,' he said. 'Faces never lie.'

'One man's good news is another's bad,' Little Horse said. He was younger. He longed to be in the thick of battle and tell stories of heroism and show off his battle scars. You could tell this just by looking at him. Younger Bear would not be this kind of warrior, he knew. But neither would he be a coward. One mistake by a coward and all the tribe could die.

'The day watchers will be waiting for us at the top,' Great Elk said. 'They will be impatient for us to arrive. We are late leaving. It is a journey of some distance.'

He led the way. Younger Bear took the middle position. Little Horse fell in behind.

'If Yellow Eagle decides—'Younger Bear called.

'Quiet!' Little Horse hissed. 'Leave space between you and Great Elk. More! More!'

'But the scouts—'

'Might not the scouts have been followed? Might not the Sioux have wiped out our watchers? Might we not be being watched at this very moment? You want to be a warrior? Then survive long enough to become one.'

Suddenly the dusk light became hazardous. The trees were no longer friendly. The spaces between bristled with the tips of arrows. A branch creaked, probably the foot of a late squirrel or an owl plumping itself awake. It could also have been the footfall of a Sioux. What might they find at the watching place? The watchers' throats cut, their scalps taken? Suddenly the gap between Younger Bear and the two warriors was a gulf. Younger Bear had never felt so alone in his life.

The slope became steeper and steeper as they climbed, the trees thinned out. Then, just as Younger Bear thought his legs would not carry him any further, they were travelling in the open, crouched below the skyline. Dusk had become darkness, darkness had become night. The stars blazed. The night was no longer young.

157

Ahead Great Elk stopped. Younger Bear stopped too and listened. At first all he could hear was his heart beating, then, when that had quietened, the sound of the wind soughing through the grass. That was all. Ahead Great Elk cautiously began to move again, sparse blade of grass by blade of grass.

The first part of night was over when they relieved the two daytime watchers, who grumbled, then left. They wanted to know what was being said back at the camp.

At first Younger Bear sat and looked down the hillsides, over the waves and ridges of the trees that led to the plain and the camps of the Sioux. Later he got tired of watching.

Little Horse threw him a cloak. 'Wrap yourself in hat,' he grunted. 'There's a hollow behind like a bed that will make you as snug as if your mother had wrapped you up herself. You'll be hidden from evil there.'

'What if I fall asleep?'

Little Horse laughed. 'That's the idea! We'll wake you when your watch comes. In any case, all this talk of Sioux—' Little Horse spat into the long grass. 'Whoever heard of a Sioux travelling at night?'

Younger Bear went to sleep.

When he woke the sky had clouded over but the moon had risen far away across the plain. He went to the edge to look down. Moonlight and darkness mixed across it like the pattern of one of the quilts his mother wove. Close to, below them, the woods were darker than ever, the moon keeping its distance.

'Sleep!' Great Elk whispered. 'Wake when you're told!'

Back in his hollow Younger Bear dreamed of playing with his childish friends. Then he dreamed of his dead father. He and his father were fighting side by side against the Sioux. He wanted to cry in his dream but his father told him he was a warrior now. Warriors were brave. He was quiet.

Later he was struck a glancing blow in the back, just enough to wake him. Without opening his eyes he knew something was wrong. Nearby Great Elk or Little Horse grunted as if he was in pain.

Younger Bear opened his eyes. Close to his face there were feet on the lip of the hollow in which he was lying. The feet stamped and searched desperately for a grip. Younger Bear glanced up. Above him Great Elk was wrestling with someone and the someone wasn't Little Horse for Younger Bear could see Little Horse lying not far away. Little Horse's eyes were open and looking at him but Little Horse was dead, with a trail of bloody spittle hanging from the corner of his mouth. The spittle dropped into the dust.

A moment later Great Elk fell to the ground. His

head tumbled into the dusty grass. For a moment he and Younger Bear stared into each other's eyes, then someone's left hand jerked the warrior's head back by the hair. A knife in a painted right hand scalped him.

Suddenly the watching place and the space around it were full of Sioux warriors. The moonlight glinted off the points of their spears and caught the colours of their painted faces and bodies. Younger Bear closed his eyes. Instinctively he knew he would be safer that way.

'Two of them?' a low voice said. 'No more? We are sure?' The words weren't exactly what his tribe would use, but most were so close Younger Bear could understand them.

'And practically asleep!' one of the Sioux laughed. Another said, 'Now they will sleep for ever!'

Younger Bear remembered how confident Little Horse and Great Elk had been that the Sioux would not come, especially by night. If that was the way Yellow Eagle thought too . . .

An older deeper voice cut in, 'Celebrate when we all have scalps on our belts. Black Kettle—' Without thinking Younger Bear opened his eyes. A young warrior, barely older than himself, stepped forward – but then almost all the Sioux seemed little older than him. 'You know the way down?'

Black Kettle nodded. 'My father took us that way many moons ago when we went to speak with Yellow Eagle.'

'Yellow Eagle,' the older voice said reflectively. 'He must be getting old. In the past he would have been better prepared than this. Lead us then. We have surprise on our side. But go carefully. I cannot believe Yellow Eagle has lost all his wiliness. If we are separated we meet back at the ponies when the sun is at its highest. Understood?'

The Sioux began to move off. Their feet kicked up the dust in Younger Bear's eyes. He was left with the watching place all to himself.

Younger Bear ran. The stitch in his side burned but the pain moved into his lungs, which felt as if they would burst, and the stitch soon became just a dull throbbing ache. In the darkness he stumbled on a stone and fell head-long. He put his hands out to save himself and his arm felt wet when he clambered to his feet but there was no time to stop and look at the injury.

He remembered Great Elk dying beside him and the anguish and surprise on Little Horse's face. He wanted to stop, to cry out with grief and horror and surprise into the darkness, but he had to keep running and running until he dropped. For long moments he forgot why he was running but he never forgot that he had to.

He was travelling down the long slope he, Great Elk and Little Horse had been looking down in the direction of the plain. At this moment he was running away from the village. If Yellow Eagle could have seen *him* he would have thought that he had chosen a coward to send up to the watching place tonight, but as soon as the Sioux had disappeared Younger Bear had had to decide. If he went back the same way as the Sioux, he could not possibly beat them to the bottom. Most likely he would not even make it that far for they would catch him blundering about among the trees and bushes in his haste to be first. What good would that do the tribe? No, he had decided to take another way that ran from the watching place to the village, a way he had stumbled on exploring at the start of summer. The only trouble was that this way was twice the distance. Could he run faster that way than the Sioux braves would creep down upon their victims?

A long ravine cut through the trees this side of the hill. Younger Bear came to the head of it. At the bottom was a stream which ran across the hillside and up which he would have to wade. It would be hard going, the slowest, worst part of the journey, wading against the icy current, but the undergrowth on the banks made it impossible to travel along them. After all his effort the stream would take him almost to within shouting distance of the tepees.

He began scrambling down the ravine. That moment the moon came back out of the clouds. She hung high in the sky ahead of him. Younger Bear lifted his arms towards her. He thanked her for lighting his way and prayed that he would reach the tepees in time to warn the tribe.

Then there was a smell that at first he could not place. He slowed down and sniffed. It was a faint smell. Then he realized what it was. Ponies! The stink of the Sioux ponies. He'd completely forgotten what the war-party leader had said.

Younger Bear stopped dead. What if the Sioux had left someone behind to guard them? What if they spotted him?

He could see the stream now far below with the moonlight mixed in with the splash of water. It beckoned him. When he splashed his feet in it he would have gone halfway. He had to take a risk of being seen. He might have been seen already. He began to run. He ran faster, faster. The stream neared. Then he tripped again. He slid, bringing an avalanche of stones with him. His head banged. He almost passed out.

Dazed, he looked back the way he'd come and there, in the moonlight, he saw two things. On the lip of the ravine, looking down, was his namesake, a bear. And making his way after him, down the way he'd come, there was a boy.

Younger Bear knelt up. At first he couldn't believe what he saw. The person running after him was himself, a boy as tall as him, as broad, his hair the same length, his twin. A moment later with a shiver he realized what was really following him. He had heard of this before, of warriors before their deaths seeing figures exactly like themselves running towards them.

Younger Bear swayed to his feet and faced the ghost. At the same time he instinctively pulled the knife that was his only weapon out of his belt. He would fight the ghost. He would not die until he had saved the tribe. The ghost slowed when it was ten paces away or so, then stopped altogether. Suddenly Younger Bear could have laughed. This was no spirit or phantom but a Sioux boy the warriors had left behind to guard their ponies.

As the boy swept his hair back out of his eyes and looked at him Younger Bear saw that they were almost identical. He'd been right – they could almost have been twins. But this boy's friends had killed his companions. He felt a surge of hatred.

As the Sioux drew his own knife Younger Bear lunged towards him. A kind of despair came over him. He realized how much depended on this. For the first time this wasn't a game. There would be no running away, no mercy for the loser. They wouldn't laugh together after and bathe each other's wounds. And this boy knew how much depended on him too. Perhaps he had a father or brother or uncle in the band that was at that moment creeping down tree by tree towards Younger Bear's camp.

Younger Bear's lunge missed. The Sioux swayed to one side and as Younger Bear stumbled against him he found himself neatly turned on the boy's hip and thrown to the ground.

The Sioux leaped at Younger Bear and stabbed at his fallen body. At the very last moment Younger Bear rolled out of the way and up to his feet.

Stalemate. They stood panting, facing each other. The Sioux feinted with his knife and Younger Bear stepped to one side as the blade came hissing in again. Younger Bear feinted in turn and stabbed. The other boy turned. They were a match. All the time the moonlight played with the edges of their blades and Younger Bear remembered how glad he'd been to see the moon come out. But the moon had shone on the other boy too and, from wherever the Sioux had been watching, shown him Younger Bear. So the Moon had shone on them both equally and fairly.

The boy's next stroke darted towards Younger Bear's face and although Younger Bear was able to turn out of its way he couldn't avoid it altogether. The edge of the blade caught him on the neck and as he straightened he knew that, even though he couldn't feel the pain, he was injured. He also realized that though he was a match for the other boy and it would be a matter of luck which one of them won, the longer he was kept here the less likely it was that his village would survive the Sioux raid. Younger Bear might win

and his family still perish. He lunged at the other boy. The desperation was his undoing. Startled, the Sioux jumped out of his way and as he did so by accident tripped Younger Bear. Younger Bear's knife flew in a long silver arc through the moonlight and into the stream.

Younger Bear sat up. The Sioux looked down at his opponent. He hadn't won yet but he knew that if he was careful he couldn't lose. He raised his knife and ran straight at Younger Bear. At the last moment, though, something behind Younger Bear caught the Sioux boy's attention. He gasped and took his eye away. It was enough. Younger Bear kicked. His opponent's knife flew through the air.

Younger Bear ran upstream. As he did so he looked back over his shoulder. The bear was lumbering away among the trees the way it had come.

Younger Bear thought the moon might not have been on his side but the animal had been. It had shaken the Sioux boy as if he'd been a doll. His broken body lay beside the water now.

Younger Bear ran. He had time yet, he thought. He would get to within shouting distance of the tepees. On the crest of the hill he would make such a cry as would raise the dead. Yellow Eagle would know what it meant.

Many thoughts went through Younger Bear's head.

He thought of the Sioux. The other boy had been younger than him but he had been a fine fighter. He would have made a fine warrior. But the bear had saved him, Younger Bear. Luck, and the bear, had been on his side.

No, not luck, Younger Bear thought. It had been a sure sign. One day he would be chief of the tribe. He knew this for certain. Maybe Yellow Eagle had known this when he sent him to the watching place tonight. He ran.

HOME
by Jonathan Kebbe

The war overtook us suddenly. I'll always remember the terrible thunder of artillery, and looking out to see flames leaping into the sky across the city.

'Go back to sleep,' my mama says, stroking my head. 'Everything's going to be fine.'

I lie listening to the explosions, and the distant howling of fire engines. Downstairs my parents arguing:

'We can return when it's all over,' my papa's saying.

'But this is our home!' Mama cries.

Papa looks in on me, kisses my brow. 'Try and sleep. We're just packing a few things in case we have to leave.'

In my dreams a great tidal wave hits the house, sweeping everything away, and I find myself clinging to my floating wardrobe, with my computer and CD player and skis bobbing by on the current.

'Hurry, Milo, get dressed!' Mama's shaking me. 'We're going!'

There's daylight in the window and terror in my mother's voice.

'But my things,' I protest.

'Never mind your things!'

'Hurry!' Papa's shouting, running down to start the Mercedes, which is packed to the roof with cases and bedding. Up and down the street neighbours are frantically clearing snow, and piling possessions and pets and themselves into cars. I can see my pal Oscar opening his gate, and we wave to each other, excited by all the madness. The air is thick with gunsmoke and danger. The world is coming apart!

In their rush to get away, neighbours are bursting out of their drives like rally drivers.

'Come on Papa!' I cry. 'You can do it!'

For an awful moment, as we race zigzagging down the icy road, I'm afraid Oscar's big red Audi is going to beat us, but Papa grits his teeth and steps on the gas and we fly into the lead!

But the contest is soon over. We were aiming to cross the river and head north to safety, but everyone else has the same idea, and soon we're stuck in a choking tide of traffic, trapped in the bright winter light with shells falling ever closer. And now there are rumours flying that the bridge is blown, and we'd better run, or fry in our cars.

I can't believe it. First we abandon our homes, now this. It isn't funny any more. My heart's sick with fear. Where are we going? What will become of us? And look at Papa, sitting at the wheel, unable to bring himself to leave his precious Merc.

'Are you crazy?' Mama's yelling at him.

A shell lands near by, splitting a tree in two, showering mud and stones. Papa grabs the valuables bag and we're running.

Then it happens. Papa has Mama's hand, and Mama has my hand, and we're stumbling down a farm track towards the shelter of a wood when – *whoosh* comes a shell, with the roar of a thousand violins, and – *bang*! My ears explode, the ground bursts under my feet, Mama's hand is torn from mine and I'm tossed through the air into darkness.

When I wake I'm in an ambulance, with an oxygen mask over my face. Next time I wake it's in hospital with a bandaged head. I don't recognize any of the faces peering down at me, and in my mind I hear myself asking the same question over and over again. But whenever I open my mouth to speak, no sound comes out.

'You're in shock,' they explain. 'You'll be fine.'

Shock has struck me dumb.

My name's Milo, I write down. *Where are my mother and father?*

'We're looking for them,' they reply. 'We'll find them soon.'

Weeks pass. They drive me to an old schoolhouse known as the 'little house of lost souls'. There are eleven of us, all sleeping in one freezing classroom, with strips of black cloth for curtains and a rusty paraffin heater.

I can't bear it, cooped up with all these strangers, no space to myself, no music of my own and none of my own clothes, only a pair of second-hand jeans and a jumper. No duvet, but a pile of musty blankets and a rock-hard pillow. And no bath, just two lukewarm showers per week in an icy temporary building.

I go round in a trance, too stunned to take it in. I keep thinking, What am I doing here? There must be some mistake. To lose your home in a war is bad enough, but both parents too . . . ? I *know* they're OK. They have to be. It's only a matter of time before they collect me.

If they don't . . . I'll curl up and die.

Some nights I wake and sit bolt upright, wondering where I am. 'Mama . . . ? Papa . . . ?'

Then my eyes make out the sleeping forms of my companions, and I know exactly where I am.

Everyone thinks I keep to myself because I'm dumb. But it's because I hate all the other kids. They're either noisy ruffians or whiny as cats. Some play normally, and then burst into tears for no reason. Me,

I haven't shed a tear. Why should I? I'm only waiting to be collected.

But as the weeks pass and winter melts into spring, my spirits sink. I lie on my bunk, refusing to attend lessons, curled up like a lifeless thing.

One big brute called Igor won't leave me alone. 'We'll see if you can talk,' he sneers, and sits on my chest, curling his fingers round my throat. 'Say you give in,' he commands. 'Say it!'

Coughing and gasping, and with tears leaping out of my eyes, I long to obey, because I'm terrified of being dead when my parents come for me. But try as I might, I can't get the words out, and I'm starting to faint when others call for help and nurses drag Igor off.

Summer fills the school with heat and light. I stand at the gate gazing down the road, waiting, waiting. It's no good fooling myself. It is just possible they may never come.

Every week or so, another one of us is called to the office. Sometimes you hear tears of sorrow, sometimes tears of relief. The kids with good news have a leaving party before rejoining their families. Those with bad news stay on, and are put up for adoption. As kids leave, new lost souls take their place. Soon there are only two of the original eleven left, me and Igor, still waiting.

On midsummer's day Igor and I are invited to the

office. I'm sick with nerves. But it's only to hear that two families are offering a vacation. A country post-man and his wife will take Igor for a week, and I'm to go to a businessman and his wife who live in a big town. And then we're to swap over for another week.

'It's a trick!' Igor reckons. 'They've decided our folks are dead and want to get rid of us.'

While Igor goes off to the country, I'm driven to a handsome street in a handsome town, through gold-tipped gates to a stately mansion. The house is even grander than my old one, and the lady who opens the door even prettier than my mother. And the garden's twice the size, with a pear-shaped pool and tennis court. As for my room, it has a pool table, computer, video and – look at that! – an indoor putting set with golf clubs.

My troubles are briefly forgotten. Mr and Mrs de Winter are very kind. They take me to the circus and cinema. Whatever I want I can have. I have space to myself, even my own bathroom. I can read or play on the computer all day long. I want to say thank you, but each time I move my lips to speak, nothing comes out but empty breath.

'It's our pleasure,' Mrs de Winter assures me. 'You see, Milo, we lost our own little boy.'

How? I ask with my eyes.

'An accident, before the war,' she replies. 'He was hit by a car. People are lost in peacetime too.'

'So it's wonderful having you,' says Mr de Winter with tears in his eyes.

When the week is over, I return for a night to the little house of lost souls, and share experiences with Igor over a game of chess.

'You're in for a shock, Milo. The postman and his wife Annie are scruffy country folk with millions of brats and a black and white TV! What about your lot?'

I put two thumbs up to say, Excellent! and then jump around miming videos, mini-golf and the pear-shaped pool.

'Swimming pool! Golf! Wow!' goes Igor. 'Now you're talking!'

Next day Igor goes to the mansion and I'm driven to a village deep in the country, pulling up before a stone cottage with cracked windows and crooked shutters and a scarecrow in the garden smoking a pipe. When I step into the dusty yard, boys and girls stop to stare, hens cluck, a goat stamps its foot on a roof, and a shabby grey dog saunters over to sniff me.

'There he is, the man himself!' greets a tall thin man in a postman's cap. 'Come along. Annie has the kettle on.'

The front door leads directly into the kitchen, where the postman's fat friendly wife is laying a table groaning with cakes and sandwiches.

''Bout time you got here,' the eldest girl, Natasha, tells me. 'We're starving!'

Then through the back door walks the scarecrow, who turns out to be the postman's dad, bearing a basket of strawberries. 'I hope you like gardening, son.' He grins. 'Your friend Igor pulled three weeds all week.'

The higgledy-piggledy house takes getting used to. I share a room with the boys, and the bathroom with everyone. Nobody owns anything, or if they do, they have to fight for it:

'Get off! That's my shirt . . . my ball . . . my banana.'

The house is leaky and draughty. The postman's forever saying, 'I must fix this, and fix that,' and Annie's forever shaking the spindrier, or thumping the TV, or stuffing socks in the windows to keep out the rain.

I'm shy and frightened. Everyone's so loud and violent, and there's no lock on the toilet door, and I can't speak even to cry out, Someone's in here! I'm afraid they think me weak and stupid, but no-one seems to care. It's 'Come on, Milo, we're off camping! We're playing soldiers! We're playing footie and you're with us.'

'No, Milo's with us!'

'Get stuffed, you had him yesterday!' They teach me to leap through flames, and make slings to shoot crows, and milk Belladonna, the bad-tempered goat. And thirteen-year-old Natasha, with her tumbling hair and brilliant eyes, invites me up to her tree-house to listen to her tapes. They don't seem to care that I can't speak. They can all work out what I'm saying: I'm not hungry . . . Shouldn't that milk be boiled? . . . Leave me alone.

Something's always happening. Even in the dead of night you're woken by excited whispers: 'Quick, we're raiding the larder!' Then, just as we get back and start gobbling our spoils – footsteps on the stairs!

'It's Dad. Quick, hide!'

Enter the postman in his pyjamas. 'What's going on in here?'

Everyone shaking with pretend fright.

'How dare you have a midnight feast,' he growls, 'without inviting me?'

Gales of laughter. The postman calls for his guitar. Natasha finds her tin whistle. Everyone else seizes anything that'll make a noise.

Enter Annie in her nightie: 'Do you lunatics know what time it is?'.

'Come on, Mum, get your fiddle.'

'Have you all gone quite mad?'

'Oh, please, Mum.'

'Oh, all right then.'

One bright morning the postman loads up his rusting hatchback and cries, 'All aboard the Orient Express!'

Everyone piles in, and I don't mind being squashed with the kids in the back, listening to their singing and joking. But when suddenly, as we're trundling through breezy countryside, the car backfires – *bang! bang!* – I think we've been hit by a shell, and nearly jump out of my skin.

'Mum, Dad, he's having a fit,' Natasha calls.

They stop the car. Annie takes me in front. I'm too old to sit on someone's lap, but I can't help myself and surrender to her arms.

'The war's far off, lad,' says the postman, driving on. 'Worst thing that can happen here is sheep wandering into the—Woah! there's one now!' and he hits the brake and swerves round the dreamy animal, tossing everyone around to shrieks of laughter.

We spend the day by the lake, swimming. Natasha plays her music, Grandad studies his birds, Annie bakes spuds in the ashes of a fire and the postman teaches me how to fish.

'Watch closely, lad. We're going to bag a perch or two for tea.'

We never catch a thing, but it's peaceful sitting with my feet in the water, and Boris the dog's chin on my knee . . . until something big and bright lands on my arm. A huge ferocious insect.

'Keep still,' murmurs the postman, 'that's an Emperor Dragonfly. You're honoured.'

Trying not to look scared; Won't it bite?

'Don't worry, it doesn't eat children. Or postmen. Only nasty people.'

I watch, fascinated, as the beautiful monster takes

178

off again, flicking back and forth over the water. I want to be that dragonfly, darting over lanes and fields in search of my parents.

Towards evening the postman rinses a jamjar, lights a candle in it and sets it floating in the water.

'Let's think for a minute about Milo's parents,' whispers Annie.

In the fading light we watch the flickering flame carrying our prayers across the lake.

The week passes in a flash.

'I'm going to miss you,' the postman says.

'We'll be here,' says Annie, 'anytime you want.'

When I get back to the little house of lost souls, Igor's eager to tell me what a rotten time he's had. The pool was too warm, the golf set too childish, the computer useless and Mr and Mrs de Winter were boring. But I sense, from his misery, that the de Winters didn't care for him much either.

A week later Igor is called to the office. He goes pale. Looks at me. Good luck! I gesture. He's in there ages. When he emerges, he sits on his bed in silence. We wait for him to spill his dreadful news. Finally, with tears running over, he says miserably, 'They're all alive, my family. I'm going to have to live with them again.'

Next day he's gone. He longed to stay, but has to return to his parents. I long to return to my parents, but I have to stay. If there is a God up there, he has a funny way of doing things.

Summer turns to autumn. I've been here nine months and never cried nor spoken. Half of me is alive, waiting to catch sight of my parents, waiting to hear their cry of *Milo!* and to feel their arms around me. Half of me is dead, dreading the worst.

There's a new crowd here now. Of the original eleven, I'm the only one left. I help the new kids to settle in, keeping a special watch over the younger ones. They all listen intently when you can't speak. Lessons in the morning – I mime – music and drama in the afternoon, games in the evening. No teasing or name-calling. Disco on Saturday and two showers per week. 'Disco' and 'showers' are fun to mime; 'Saturday' and 'per week' is tricky.

November rain lashes the windows. My mind wanders. I remember kind Mr and Mrs de Winter, and the jolly postman's family, and I think I'd like to see them all again.

One day a nurse taps my shoulder. Dr Linden wants to see me in the office. My legs go weak. I head for her office like a sleepwalker. Stand trembling at her door. I daren't go further. But I must. My hand rises to knock.

'It's about your parents . . .' she says, and hurries on in case I think it's good news. I know by her expression that it's not, and you can see she dreads telling me.

'I'm afraid the news is bad, Milo.'

I watch her mouth forming the words. For a few seconds more I'll cling to the hope that Mama and Papa are captured, or injured, but alive. Or maybe one is dead and one alive. I've sometimes pondered, lying awake at night, which one I'd rather have survive, my mother or father, if one of them had to be dead . . .

Dr Linden takes a deep breath. 'Milo, you're going to have to be very brave . . .'

Brave? Why should I be brave?

'I'm afraid they're dead,' she says.

Dead.

The word hangs in the room.

Dead.

Over and over it rings in my brain, and still I can't grasp it, like a ball bouncing out of my hands.

'They were shot, Milo. In a prison camp. It would have been very quick.'

I picture my parents tied to a post, or facing a wall like naughty children, bullets punching holes in them, the blood coming out. I can't bear it, thinking of them lifeless on the ground, never to get up again, never to hug each other, or tuck me in. To think I'll never see them again. Ever. I try to picture their murderers, mean laughing men, too stupid to know how precious life is. You can't take other people's lives. You're not allowed to. But since they have, I want to kill them. I want to see them dead on the ground with their blood running out.

Nurses take turns sitting with me at night. Perhaps they expect me to cry, but I've forgotten how to. Day after day I go round like a ghost. I refuse to feel a thing. I'm a robot.

Dr Linden finds me one morning in the vegetable patch, planting strawberries for next year: 'Milo, how would you feel about choosing a new family?'

I look up from my work. What's she talking about?

'Remember the two families you spent a week with? They've both expressed an interest in adopting you as their son.'

I gaze at her blankly. Why would I want another family? What's wrong with mine?

'Well, what do you think?'

It's now that it really hits me.

My mama and papa are dead. Do you understand, Milo? You will never see them again. You're on your own.

My eyes well up and spill over. Dr Linden catches me in her arms.

That night, after I've stopped blubbing, I ask her in mime where my parents are.

'In a great big grave, Milo . . . with lots of others.'

But are they in Heaven? – I point to the sky.

'Yes, I'm sure they are.'

Days later I'm packing a bag and combing my hair, and Dr Linden drives me to that handsome street in that handsome town, through the gold-tipped gates to the mansion. Mr and Mrs de Winter are pleased to see me. A little too pleased, I'm thinking: 'Will you have another cake, Milo? Have some more Coke, Milo. Would you like us to send you to the best school? And to appoint the best doctors to help you speak again? Would you like to stay with us?'

Mrs de Winter tucks me in. Kisses me goodnight.

I lie very still. My body feels strange, as if it doesn't belong to me. As the night moves on, the moon runs a long slow finger over the wonders of my room — the silent CD player and computer, the rigid golf clubs and the frozen surface of the pool table, all lifeless things, dead things.

The huge beautiful house is quiet. Dead quiet. I've grown used to the infuriating and comforting racket of other kids.

Mrs de Winter opens my curtains. 'Good morning, Milo! Shall we have breakfast together?'

I pick at my food.

'Where's your appetite, dear? You must eat to grow big and strong. Then what would you like to do today? We've heated the pool specially.'

I want to make a phone call, I mime.

She looks puzzled. Why would I want to make a phone call?

I take out my little pad: *Dr Linden's number, please.*

'Dr Linden's number? Why on earth do you want Dr Linden's number? *I'm* here to take care of you. If there's anything you need, you only have to ask.'

Too panicky to remember my manners, I wave my pad at her.

'And anyway, you can't speak, so how can you make a phone call?'

I can! I can! I say with my face.

'Oh really!' she says crossly, fetching the number, but determined to dial it herself.

'I can't imagine what's the matter, Doctor,' she says when finally she gets through, 'after all we're doing to make him happy.'

I hold out my hand for the phone.

'Milo?' Dr Linden's voice. 'What's the matter?'

I want to say, Look, I'm very grateful for all they're doing, and the pool's great and everything, *but I hate it here. Come and get me!* Instead, all I manage is a string of wheezes and teary grunts.

She understands, and arrives two hours later to take me back to the little house of lost souls. Such relief. I can breathe again. I'm not Mr and Mrs de Winter's little boy. I'm not anybody's little boy any more.

'You can stay with us as long as you wish,' says Dr Linden. 'You more or less run the place anyway. I don't know what we'd do without you! But . . .' She smiles. 'If you feel like visiting the postman's family . . .'

Days later we head for the cottage in the country. When we pull up in the puddly yard, the goat stamps, the old man waves from the garden and the kids come running in woolly hats and thump me:

'Come on, Milo, we've kicked off and you're in goal!'

Natasha appears, hands on hips. 'Well, Stranger, what kept you? Aren't we good enough for you?'

She grabs me and pushes me indoors. The postman ruffles my hair. Annie gives me a warm hug. 'My! You're growing fine and tall.'

Outside I can hear the hens clucking and the kids shrieking.

Where's Boris? I mime, remembering the old grey dog who used to rest his chin in my lap.

'He died,' Annie sighs, 'peacefully in his sleep.'

'I'll leave you for a few days, Milo,' says Dr Linden. 'Call me, and I'll collect you sooner.'

That night I lie listening to the boys fooling and arguing, and Annie coming in to scold. In the morning there's the usual chaos of breakfast, and then I set off with the postman in his little orange van, village to village, delivering the mail. In the afternoon I help Grandad prune the plum tree, chop kindling wood for Annie, and meet the kids returning from school across the fields.

Days pass. It begins to snow. The snow paints lines near and far in furrows and tractor tracks, and then covers the entire canvas of the land. It covers the cottage, the garden, and Boris's grave, with its little headstone carved by the kids. It's probably right now covering the deep ground where my parents lie.

Dr Linden arrives one afternoon. I didn't call her, but I'm glad to see her. She stays for a cup of tea. The kids come in from the cold, stamping snow off their boots.

'I think it's decision time, Milo,' says Dr Linden gently.

Decision time. My heart races.

'We all like you, Milo,' Annie says. 'You're welcome to come for holidays, or to stay for good. You're free to choose.'

The flames crackle in the grate. The wind whines in the chimney.

I'm free to choose.

I'm free.

'Are you staying?' Dr Linden finishes her tea. 'Or coming with me?'

Dr Linden's worn out. I'm not the only lost soul in the world.

I rise from my seat and cross the room murmuring something.

'What was that?' Natasha blurts. 'Milo said something!'

I take Annie's hand, and reach for the postman's hand. Then I take another breath and out it comes, clear as a bell:

'Home.'

The word hovers over our heads like the first word ever spoken.

AMAZING ADVENTURE STORIES

Collected by TONY BRADMAN

I almost laughed out loud. Except that pistol was wavering all over the room. Then it suddenly went off . . .

Ever wondered what you would do if you came face to face with a Nazi parachutist in the Second World War, or were held hostage in the middle of nowhere for your dad's riches? What if you were marooned on a desert island on your way to Australia? Or caught up with a murderess?

Tony Bradman has collected ten action-packed adventure stories from a team of top authors such as Malorie Blackman, Robert Westall, Douglas Hill and Helen Dunmore in this fast-moving and gripping anthology. Your nerves will never be the same again!

'Excitement, fear and suspense in equal measure . . . all the stories are thoroughly entertaining' *School Librarian*

0 552 52768 8

SENSATIONAL CYBER STORIES

Collected by TONY BRADMAN

Boot up your imagination and log in to this sensational collection of cyber stories.

A bit of hacking for fun goes seriously wrong when a rogue computer program sends out the secret police to arrest the school boy hackers; a boy swaps his brain with his computer's memory, and amazes all his friends with his command of facts and figures; and virtual reality becomes blurred in a thrilling but dangerous game . . .

Ten incredible stories involving state-of-the-art technology and real human excitement from top children's authors including Malorie Blackman, Helen Dunmore and Paul Stewart. Guaranteed to tempt even the most addicted game-player away from the computer screen!

0 552 54525 2

FANTASTIC SPACE STORIES

Collected by TONY BRADMAN

10,9,8,7,6,5,4,3,2,1 . . . We have lift off!

In this fantastic new collection of space stories, you'll travel on board Starskimmer 1 the galaxy-flying starship, experience life in a Martian colony, be trapped inside the cavernous guts of a bubble – and undergo a serious sky-jacking in deepest, darkest outer space!

Blast off into other galaxies of aliens, patrol-droids, stun-guns and koptas, in these ten gripping stories by authors including Nicholas Fisk, Malorie Blackman, Helen Dunmore, Douglas Hill and Mary Hoffman. An anthology that's truly out of this world!

'A first-class collection' *School Librarian*

0 552 52767 X

FOOTBALL FEVER

Collected by TONY BRADMAN

Go for goal with these exciting and action-packed soccer stories!

Take a grandstand seat for some great soccer action: a barefoot boy who beats the odds and amazes everyone with his stunning skills; a goalie called Titch, who proves height isn't everything when it comes to saving goals; and the one and only Harry Jackson, determined to be the best referee ever.

Tony Bradman has collected ten brand-new, action-packed tales for this terrific collection of never-before-published football stories from a team of top children's authors including Rob Childs, Nick Warburton and Geraldine McCaughrean. All the fun, the drama, the action and excitement of the football field is here, so kick off into the world of football fever!

0 552 52974 5